905

STANLEY BALDWIN

SERVICE OF OUR LIVES

LAST SPEECHES AS PRIME MINISTER

HODDER AND STOUGHTON
ST. PAUL'S HOUSE, LONDON, E.C.4

First published   .   .   .   .   .   . June, *1937*
Eighth Edition (*first in this form*) .   .   *1938*

Made and Printed in Great Britain for Hodder and Stoughton Limited,
by Butler & Tanner Ltd. Frome and London

PUBLISHERS' NOTE

THIS FOURTH VOLUME OF THE SPEECHES AND
addresses of Mr. Stanley Baldwin aims to complete the record in book form of his principal
public utterances as a national leader.

The last speech included in *This Torch of
Freedom* was delivered during the General
Election of 1935. The period here covered is
that last momentous year and a half during
which he remained the First Minister of the
Crown.

The Publishers' grateful acknowledgments
are due to *The Times*, The British Broadcasting
Corporation and *The Listener*, *The Methodist
Recorder*, *Berrow's Worcester Journal*, The
Executive Council of The Universities Bureau
of the British Empire ; and to The Controller
of His Majesty's Stationery Office for permission to follow the text of the Official Reports
of the Parliamentary Debates in the speeches
beginning on pp. 11, 32, 82, 103 and 151.

LET US DEDICATE OURSELVES — let us dedicate ourselves afresh, if need be — to the service of our fellows, a service in widening circles, service to the home, & service to our neighbourhood, to our county, our province, to our country, to the Empire, and to the world. No mere service of our lips, service of our lives, as we know will be the service of our King and Queen. God bless them.

CONTENTS

9

CONTENTS

ON A MEMORIAL TO ADMIRAL OF THE FLEET EARL JELLICOE

Speech delivered in the House of Commons,
December 12, 1935

I BEG TO MOVE:

" That this House will, to-morrow, resolve itself into a Committee to consider an humble Address to His Majesty, praying that His Majesty will give directions that a monument be erected at the public charge to the memory of the late Admiral of the Fleet Earl Jellicoe, as an expression of the admiration of this House for his illustrious naval career and its gratitude for his devoted services to the State."

I think it might be for the convenience of those who have not been long in the House if I remind them, as I reminded Members on that occasion six years ago when I moved a similar Resolution with regard to Lord Haig, of what it is that this Resolution effects. In effect the House pledges itself to honour the Estimate which will in due course be presented for the work sanctioned by the House under the Resolution. When that Estimate is presented the full amount involved will be shown to the House, and according to precedent the figure that comes in the Estimate will be one somewhere in the neighbourhood of £6,000; it may be rather more or it may be rather less.

With those preliminary words on business I would desire to take a short time this afternoon in moving this Motion and justifying it to the House and to the country. As I observed six years ago, these occasions are not the time for estimating or attempting to estimate the ultimate position which may be held by the great man whose memory we desire to perpetuate. As I have often said, whether a man be a soldier or a sailor or a statesman the position he may ultimately occupy in the view of historians or in the regard of his countrymen is not one which can be estimated even approximately in his lifetime. But it is the duty of each generation, surely, to pay its tribute to those who, in their view and so far as they are able to judge, may deserve well of the State; and such a one—I say it without fear of contradiction as I said it of Lord Haig —was Lord Jellicoe.

Again, this is not the occasion to dwell at any length on his professional career, beyond saying that his whole life, viewed in the light of later events, seemed to have been a fitting preparation for what he had to do and what he accomplished. His whole life was devoted to the service of his profession, and for that service he kept both body and mind in training and in subjection, so that when the time came and at whatever age it might find him, he at any rate, so far as all he could do, would be ready to respond to the call, and would respond.

It is not for me to estimate how much that modern Navy, as it was when the Great War began, owed in its technical development and its efficiency to Lord Jellicoe and to the men with whom he worked. The country at large knew little of what went on in those pre-War days in the Services. Suffice it for us to remember that Lord Jellicoe was working long with Lord Fisher on those reforms both in material and in personnel which left so strong and deep a mark upon the senior Service. Suffice it for us to remember that Lord Jellicoe was working with Sir Percy Scott at the time when they were attempting to concentrate so much of the effort of the scientific Navy to improving the gunnery of the whole Service. He was with Sir Percy Scott at the time of the introduction of director firing, and he himself in the natural course of his duties raised the Atlantic Fleet three years before the War from the lowest place to the highest place in the Navy in its gunnery, and he performed the same service a year later to the Battle Squadron of the Home Fleet.

Then came the Great War. Most of us have hardly yet begun to realize how infinitely remote the problems of that War were from the Napoleonic wars whose history was so familiar to us, whose romantic history must have appealed to all of us older men in the days of our youth. The kind of work that was done in the Napoleonic times by so many ships and by fleets was work that in the Great War fell much more to smaller portions of the Fleet and to the smaller ships. The great task of the Commander-in-Chief was to take over, as he did, the whole fleets of the Empire and to weld them together into one great homogeneous unit, on which the whole fate of the Empire and of these islands depended for four years. He obtained and maintained the undisputed command of the sea before, during and after the Battle of Jutland. His was the controlling and directing mind of the greatest assembly of naval power that the world has ever seen, and very possibly that the world will ever see. The trust reposed in him was a tremendous trust. The responsibility was perhaps the greatest single responsibility on any man in the War. All of us who were at home at that time were sheltered behind the Grand Fleet, and we were able to go on with our work as no other people in Europe were, without any fear or apprehensions lest our soil might be the soil on which the invader fought our own people. We had our cares, our sorrows, our troubles, but from that anxiety, from which no people in Europe was free, we were free, and we were free because of the Grand Fleet.

It was a Grand Fleet which, in spite of innumerable difficulties and innumerable perils, succeeded in keeping this country fed, and the measure of these things is the measure of the burden that lay upon the shoulders of the man who was in command of that Fleet. We ask much more of our seamen in our island home than is asked of their seamen by any other country in the world, and that which we asked was given to us, and the trust we reposed in our seamen and in their great leader was justified from the first day of the War until the Armistice. In him we are honouring a worthy successor of the great and immortal line of British seamen.

Now let me remind you, if you have forgotten it—it leads me naturally to what I want to say about the man—that when the Lord

Mayor of London went up in his official capacity to visit the Grand Fleet on behalf of the citizens of London he made an observation which I would like to bring back to the recollection of the House. He said that he went up in what he described as one of the grimmer phases of the War, and he added:

"Fogs and rough seas surrounded our physical presence, but Jellicoe himself was a beacon of hope and confidence."

Those were great words to write of any man at that time, and I would ask you to remember with them some words which I read in a letter by a distinguished Naval officer who was a midshipman in the Fleet in 1916. He wrote thus:

"My lasting impression is of the personal influence diffused by the Commander-in-Chief. None of us had ever spoken to him; many of us had never seen him; but so closely had he identified himself with the day-to-day duties of every man in the Fleet that we all felt as if we were serving in the Flagship. Jellicoe was the Grand Fleet."

17

This is an amazing thing for a lad to say. How does it come about? No one can explain it. It is that God-given gift of personality which is a form of manifestation of genius and is inexplicable, for it cannot be taught by book-learning, it cannot be acquired merely by a desire to obtain it. A man has it or he has not; and that great gift was Jellicoe's. Perhaps it may help to explain it when I remind the House that Jellicoe was a man of deep religious conviction. He was a man of wonderful understanding of the human heart. He was kindly and thoughtful to everyone of every kind, in every rank, with whom he was brought into contact, and he had in full measure that gift of inspiring with affection all who worked with him and for him, and with that, and an absolutely concomitant part of it, a flawless sincerity and complete selflessness. He was loved by every officer and man who served with him.

There is only one observation I would make in conclusion. It has often seemed, in reading history, that perhaps the happiest death, and the death that helps to secure immortality for a man, is the death that comes to him in the moment of his greatest achievement. Such were the deaths of Wolfe and of Nelson in the hour of victory, and no less famous the death of Richard Grenville in the hour of defeat, and the names of those men will live as long as stories of human achievement and chivalry and daring can stir the human heart. But for Haig and for Jellicoe it was reserved to see many years of life, when the peak of their achievement was passed, and surely, if ever, those are the testing years of character. With neither of those men, in those last years, was there the slightest deviation from the lives they had always led, lives in which duty always came first, the duty that lay to hand.

Jellicoe, as Haig, passed from one of the most prominent positions in the whole world to the position of a private citizen. From neither of them did you ever hear a word of criticism or reproach of anything connected with themselves, their own careers, what people said about them. They had played their part and they were content to leave history to judge. They devoted themselves as long as they had strength to the service of the men who had worked side by side with them through those years of the War, and to both of them came a merciful and peaceful end. They were allowed some years of peace, but years in which they enjoyed health to work. Each was called away in the full possession of his powers after a short and comparatively painless illness. And so, in our controversial life in politics, in the strenuous work of trying to govern successfully and happily our common country, it is well, I think, to turn aside on such an occasion as this, if it be only for a moment, that we may think of Lord Jellicoe and all that he stood for to the nation, and all that he stands for as an example to every man that loves his country, a man whose single aim through life was the public service and the service of his fellow men and who, throughout his life, worked with a fine resolution and with a lovely humanity, and whose passing we now mourn. A great sailor, sir, and a great man.

ON THE DEATH OF KING
GEORGE THE FIFTH

Speech broadcast from London,
January 21, 1936

" AFTER HE HAD SERVED HIS OWN GENERATION
BY THE WILL OF GOD HE FELL ON SLEEP AND
WAS LAID UNTO HIS FATHERS."

Those words kept recurring to me in the
watches of last night, for if there was one thing
that our King had done it was to serve his own
generation by the will of God, and because of
that the news of the death of His Majesty, when
it came, has been heard everywhere with a
personal grief, not only in this country, but
through the vast Empire over which he
bore rule, and, I believe, far beyond its
borders.

To famous men all the earth is a sepulchre.
It is less than a month ago that the voice now

silent was heard around the world, a King addressing his subjects, a father seated with his family speaking to his people, members of his wider family, words of wisdom, courage, and deep human sympathy. And it is as members of a family that we are mourning him to-day. There must be millions who feel as I do that a wise and loving friend and counsellor has been taken from us, and for long the world will seem a poorer and a colder place without him, and the tones of that well-known voice are echoing in our ears to-day as our thoughts turn to the widowed Queen and to the bereaved family.

And I do want to say a word to you about Queen Mary, for I know that every heart in the Empire is sore for her this night. It often seems to me that in a married life so perfect, so happy, as theirs was, there has to come that inevitable day when one is taken and the other is left, and one of the two has to continue the pilgrimage to the end alone. There are millions of hands which, if they could reach the Queen, would be stretched out to her and tears of sympathy be shed with her; and it must be some comfort to her, though we cannot tell her that, to know of that feeling, and she must know it from the events of that wonderful Jubilee summer. But may not this be a comfort to her as it has been a comfort to others, that, after all, the one who is left is really carrying the cross for the one who has gone before?

If she were not suffering to-day, he would be, and she is bearing what might have been his sorrow for him; and I cannot help feeling that with a King, knowing how lonely the high places of the world are, and knowing that he has no one but his wife with whom he might have really intimate converse—I tremble to think what it might have been for him had he been alone in his awful task with no voice by him to cheer, to comfort, and to encourage. We are thankful indeed to feel that even in her sorrow Queen Mary is spared to the people who love her, and I am sure that we all of us, all our people, will show her in whatever way they can how close she is to their hearts, and

how they will treasure her not only for the
King's sake but for her own.

And as to the King, what can I say in a few
minutes, and within twenty-four hours of this
shattering blow? I think I may dwell for
these few minutes on the King as I have known
him during this last year, and try to picture
him as one who has borne the responsibilities
of his position during perhaps the most difficult
quarter of a century in which a monarch has
ever sat on our Throne.   There was no respite
for him during those twenty-five years.   The
whole world has been in a state of commotion,
and there never seemed to come to him any
period when he could look ahead for two or
three years and feel that all would be peace
and quiet, and nothing in the world to cause
him or his people trouble.   The world has been
what a great man of the sixteenth century
called it, "a raving world," and he played
his part in it gallantly to the end, and I do feel
most thankful that after that illness of his six
years ago he was spared to see that Jubilee
year.

24

He and his Ministers and his doctors and, I think, all who knew much about these things, felt some apprehension as to the strain he might have to undergo in attending the various ceremonies and functions that belonged to that time. But all our fears were belied, for there seemed to be given to him a special strength to go through those weeks. And I rejoice that he, modest as ever, diffident as to his own powers, often wondering what his people thought of what he had done and tried to do for them—I often think that it was a most wonderful experience for him to see, to have brought home to him, that all he had done had sunk deep into their hearts. The occasion of that Jubilee was the occasion that they all embraced to throw off that shyness so characteristic of us, and show him openly and without shame that they were proud of him as their King, that they loved him as a man.

The effect on him, I think, was great. He never referred to it without emotion. He was profoundly touched. He accepted that tribute with a thankful humility. I am indeed thankful

that he lived to see it, and that during the last
months he knew what he meant to his people.
But we knew that there was no strength
to spare. To go through that last illness had
taken from him every reserve of strength that
he had. We knew that it must go hard with
him if any illness should attack him, even were
it a slight one, and I myself noticed in the
months that followed the Jubilee—and I have
never known him so gentle, so calm—an
increase even of his customary consideration,
his customary kindliness, and I had a feeling,
which I expressed to my friends, through all
the autumn, that he was ready for the long
journey that he was so soon to take.

He was tired at times, and I used to contrast
his lot with the lot of the politicians, for we
can and do have our old age, if we live, to
ourselves. But the King's burden is never
lifted. It goes on all through the year, and it
goes on with age, and the only release from it
is death. And then, again, you will remember
the death of his sister. Many who are listening to me to-night may be elderly brothers and

sisters, perhaps between sixty and seventy years of age. You know what a link that is, the common memories of childhood, and there are few losses as men and women get older, few losses that strike so deep as those of contemporary relations with their share of common memories. And it was no ordinary bond, no formal bond, that united the King and his sister. They were devoted to each other, and his Majesty, if he had not seen her, would talk to her on the telephone every night and tell her what he had been doing, to cheer her and make her life less lonely. I think that he felt the severance of that old tie very keenly.

I saw him for the last time when we parted for the Christmas holidays. It is the only time in the year that I am able to go to my own home, and he was going to his at Sandringham, and we were rejoicing together, for we both loved the same kind of holiday, and we were going to spend it with our own children and with our grandchildren at our own home in the country. It was but a few days after that when the first intimation reached us that all was not well. At the end of last week and during the week-end I was in constant touch with Sandringham, and it was only yesterday morning the King's secretary rang me up to tell me that he had seen a change, and that he feared that the end could not be long delayed.

There is one thing I think I can tell you without any impropriety, for though much, and indeed most, of what passes near the end is sacred, and we none of us have the desire or right to inquire into what happened at those times, yet I think I may tell you this. The King was having brief intervals of consciousness, and each time he became conscious it was some kind of inquiry or kind observation of someone, some words of gratitude for kindness shown. But he did say to his secretary when he sent for him: "How is the Empire?" An unusual phrase in that form, and the secretary said: "All is well, sir, with the Empire," and the King gave him a smile and relapsed once more into unconsciousness.

It was simply this, that during all that time subconsciously and just coming to the surface at odd moments was that same love for his people, care for their well-being here and throughout the world, for that family to whom he spoke last Christmas, and the thought of them was with him to the end. King George, it is true, inherited his position on the Throne, but he won his own way to the hearts of his people. Behind the pomp and the pageantry incidental to his great position he laboured night and day in that high station to which God had called him. The doing of his duty to the utmost of his ability was the guiding principle of his life.

Great power which corrupts weak natures ennobled our King's character and made him subdue passion and will and energy to his duty to his country. He brought the dispositions that are lovely in private life into the service and conduct of the Commonwealth, and not only in virtue of his office but in virtue of his person was he the first gentleman in the land. As the knowledge of the King's complete dedication to duty grew and spread as his reign proceeded, so did the respect of his people turn into reverence, and reverence into love. It is literally true that he won their hearts and during the Jubilee they made that manifest to him.

This is the truth we must bear in mind as we think of the son who succeeds to the Throne and upon whom has now fallen one of the heaviest burdens that can rest upon the shoulders of fallible and mortal man. We can best honour the noble memory of King George by gathering round and sustaining the young King whom for so long we have delighted to know as the Prince of Wales. All eyes are upon him as he advances to his father's place, and, while he is no stranger to public duty, he is now summoned to face responsibilities more onerous, more exacting, more continuous, than any he has hitherto been asked to discharge.

He comes to them in the prime of his powers, and already known throughout the length and breadth of his Empire. His great gifts of mind and heart he is now called upon to consecrate to his people. He inherits an example of kingly conduct, of virtue, of wisdom, and of endurance. King George's reign was marked by far-reaching constitutional and Parliamentary changes without precedent in our long history. He earned the loyalty and respect of all parties in the State, new and old. He hands down in turn to his son the throne he himself received from his father, and he hands it down with its foundations strengthened, its moral authority, its honour, and its dignity enhanced. It is an incomparable and awe-inspiring inheritance.

The young King knows the confidence we all repose in him. He knows that he commands not only the allegiance, he knows that the understanding, the affection, and the prayers of the countless multitudes of his subjects are with him at this hour. May God guide him aright and God Save the King.

ON A MEMORIAL TO ADMIRAL
OF THE FLEET EARL BEATTY

Speech delivered in the House of Commons,
May 5, 1936

FOR THE SECOND TIME WITHIN A FEW MONTHS
the House is being asked by me to pass a
Motion of this description. I know it will
gratefully pass this Motion for a permanent
memorial to the late Admiral of the Fleet Earl
Beatty, as an expression of its sense of
gratitude to the second of the two great sailors
who bore on their shoulders the immense
responsibility of command in the Great War.
For nearly half the Great War Lord Beatty
served under Lord Jellicoe. From November,
1916, until the end of the War he bore upon
his shoulders that almost intolerable responsibility, the chief responsibility for the safety of
our country. They were both great sailors,
different of course, but those differences may

well be explored by the historians. For me and for the House to-day, we seek not to compare the measure, but merely to express our thankfulness that at the time of our country's need two such men as Jellicoe and Beatty were there to respond to the call.

As a sailor he was undoubtedly a figure which appealed to the imagination of the British people. There is no doubt that to our people, whether they live on the sea coast, in the great towns, or inland, the Royal Navy is in some subtle way the repository of the spirit and the tradition of our nation; and there is no doubt that instinctively our people seemed to recognize in Lord Beatty the sure successor to those men whose names were so familiar to them and whose sayings have almost passed into the conversation of our land. We think of Duncan, off the Texel, who, when he had taken soundings, said: " There is depth of water enough, and if the *Venerable* should sink, her flag would show at the masthead." We think of Grenville who, dying, gave orders to scuttle his ship with all on board her lest she should fall into the hands of the Spaniards. We think of Raleigh driving his little ships into Cadiz harbour and answering the guns of the Spanish forts with an insolent flourish of trumpets. We think of Nelson at the Nile, when he saw the ship of his great friend Troubridge run aground and he commiserated him, " while his more fortunate companions were in the full tide of happiness "; and at Copenhagen when he said, as the battle began: " It is warm work and this may be the last of us at any moment, but, mark you, I would not be elsewhere for thousands."

When one thinks of these things one feels instinctively how Beatty might have taken his stand by any of these Admirals, and how, had he been in their place, what they said would have sprung naturally to his lips. In Beatty, fighting his battles as he did from an exposed position which he selected for himself on the compass platform high above the bridge, calm, unruffled and alert, our people rightly saw the embodiment of that persisting spirit of the

34

Royal Navy that has lasted through the
centuries and has been the glory of the Navy
and the pride of our country, an inspiration
not only to the men who served with him but
to the people of this country through the
darkest days.

When I think of Beatty as the people thought
of him, I like to think of another aspect of
him familiar to me but much less familiar to
his countrymen. Although a public figure,
although gifted with all those qualities that
attract the admiration of mankind, spectacular
qualities we might call them in some ways, yet
the man himself was fundamentally a shy man,
a man who disliked publicity, who never
courted it, and who, I rejoice to think, took no
part in any of the controversies that have raged
since the War. He kept himself aloof from all
those things. Men who worked with him
have often told me of the deep impression made
on them by his foresight, by his method and
by the gift of sheer hard work that he brought
to his profession, all of which things were
precedent to the prompt decision and the

35

vigorous action for which the world knew him so well.

Those qualities and a mind attuned to statesmanship were given in full after the War, when he spent more than seven years at the Admiralty at a time of intense difficulty for any First Sea Lord, at a time when in the hands of any lesser man it might have been impossible to have accomplished what was done in the way it was done; for this great sailor, who had been in command of the greatest naval force the world has ever seen, had in those years immediately succeeding the War to turn the whole of his influence, the whole of his knowledge and the whole of his skill, to reducing that force to the very skeleton of what it had been, to see that after those reductions what was left was as efficient as it could be, on that comparatively slender scale, to see that all the changes of personnel that had to be made, the dismissals, were done—hardship there must have been in many cases—with as little hardship as was possible. These things he did and he served four or five separate Governments,

all with the same devotion to duty and
with the same loyalty. Those last years
of his service to his country showed a
man no less great in any way than he had
been at the height of his power with the Grand
Fleet.

When that work was done, for a short time
he enjoyed such rest as was more than due to
him, but in those last months, in failing health,
there were two calls of personal duty to which
he with his nature would not fail to respond.
He followed his brother admiral, Lord Jellicoe,
to his grave, and later, on the occasion when
most of us saw him for the last time and were
struck only too sadly by his appearance, he
followed his beloved King on the last march
through London. His gallant spirit is now at
rest and it only remains for this House, as they
will, to pay him with no dissentient voice that
tribute that they reserve for men who have
rendered superlative service to their country.
There can be no greater honour to any man
than that this House, as I have said on one
previous occasion, should stand aside for a few

brief moments from its constant strife and unite to pay its tribute to those who have deserved well of the State. This, I am convinced to-day, we shall all do as one man in this House.

ON THE NEW WORLD WAITING
FOR THE NEW SCHOOLBOY

Speech delivered at the Leys School, Cambridge,
June 26, 1936

AS THE ELOQUENT SENIOR PREFECT IN HIS
admirable speech preferred the request for a
whole holiday, I remembered reading some
beautiful words in the School Magazine. They
contain so profound a truth that I feel a school
which can produce a boy capable of writing
such words deserves not a day but a month's
holiday. "English politicians," he writes,
"have as much sense as those of all other
nations put together." With these words
ringing in my ears I had a communication on
the nod with the head master, and the petition
is granted.

It gives me great pleasure to come here for
many reasons. One of them is that I make
my appearance at the same time as my old

friend, Sir Josiah Stamp, makes his first appearance as your Chairman. Twenty years ago, as Financial Secretary to the Treasury, I had to deal with War Budgets—a dismal subject; and one part of it was the most dismal and complicated, the question of excess profits. I remember once saying to the House of Commons: "It is quite true I have not the least idea what this clause means, but I can assure you that it is all right"; and they passed the clause without a division! That assurance was given by Sir Josiah Stamp, so I felt sure of my ground.

Sir Josiah hinted that one of the things that attracted me to this function was that it was a Speech Day. That is all wrong. When my time comes to an end in public life, for whatever years may then be spared to me, I hope my epitaph may be written in a slight paraphrase of some well-known words of Tennyson's: "He made no speeches—no, nor listened to them."

I remember when I was at school, and people made speeches to us, I was struck by two things. I was struck by the age of the speakers —I always thought they came out of the Ark—and I was struck by their lack of any intimate knowledge of the environment in which I lived.

There was one piece of " peculiar bilge " which old gentlemen were very apt to speak on such occasions as the present; and that was that one's school days were the happiest time of one's life.

It is difficult to cram more fallacies into so short a sentence. As a matter of fact, for most men it is not true. Many boys do enjoy their school days enormously and perhaps can say, with as much honesty as a man can say on looking back forty years, that they were the happiest times of their life. But it is not really so with most boys, because the whole process, I think, of becoming a man is a very difficult one.

I find in looking back on my life, which now, I am sorry to say, is nearly seventy years (incredible as it is for me to think), that it has been progressively happier, far more interesting as time has gone on, for all its cares and all its anxieties. After all the uneasy and unsatisfied stretchings after a dim and unknown future which so many boys go through at school are over, there will come, with the adjustment of oneself and with finding one's feet in the world, a much happier frame of mind than that experienced at school. There are exceptions; good athletes, for example, are perhaps happiest at school. But for the majority the best days are afterwards.

It is very difficult to realize the completely different world in which you are living from the world in which I and my generation lived at your age. We had a sense of security, stability and certainty. When we read history and learned of the movements and clash of nations, we thought that was all finished and that nothing like it could happen again. The War changed all that.

You must remember, too, that most of us lived in the country. There are very few people living in the country to-day in that sense. We lived at the centre of a circle whose radius was ten miles—the distance a horse could take us and bring us back. We never went away for week-ends, because we could not. Don't think we were not happy; we had a thundering good time. In the present age the time has gone when you will get a class of people who have lived all their lives in the country. England is being urbanized fast, and this has affected your generation.

I have often thought of the tragedy that may come about in two or three generations, when a time will come in which our great literature will be of less value, because all similes drawn from the land and from sailing ships will have to be explained to those who read them. Indeed what I fear is that half our ancient literature may be unintelligible to future generations on account of their inability to understand such similes.

For the present generation everything is a matter of speed. Speed has become the god of our modern civilization. You have got to adapt yourselves to it, but don't think it is synonymous with civilization. It took sixteen days for news of Trafalgar to reach London; a generation or two ago, it took three weeks for dispatches from our Ambassadors abroad to reach the Government. To-day the cables of the whole world are throbbing day and night between the capitals of the world and London, mostly with serious news. Before a cable from your representative at Tokyo has been decoded, the telephone rings and the Japanese Ambassador is asking for your explanation.

Where is the time for consideration and reflection? That very fact may account for some of the mistakes made in the world in late years. The awful problem, which I cannot hope to solve, is: Can the capacity of the human mind grow to meet the need which modern speed requires?

The age of stability has become an age of mutability. Many of you boys are students of history and may have studied the latter half of the seventeenth century. It has often struck me that there is a very close analogy between that period and the days we are living in. At the end of the seventeenth century, history had its roots in the Civil War. Englishmen longed for constitutional stability. Being English, they did not solve their problems logically. (Logic is all right for the French, but when an Englishman gets logical he becomes absolutely hopeless for practical life.) They got their solution in the reign of Queen Anne.

To-day in the same way we have got our roots in the thoughts and ideas that came up immediately after the War. I think we went through half a century of political evolution during the War, and came out of it before any of us were ready for the new conditions. In the next few years there will be, and must be, a lot of experimenting; and I hope that the amazing instinct of our people, that hammered out a way to salvation in those far off difficult days, may be relied on to bring us through now. That instinct is to do the right thing at the right time. No one knows exactly where the new world is going. We are feeling our way as our ancestors did at that time; but I have every hope we shall find our way.

45

In days to come, it is to boys like you that England must look for the fellows who are going to lead the country through. You will be going into all sorts of vocations—Business, the Professions, the Ministry, possibly Politics. Whatever it is, don't think too much of yourselves or your career. Take your job and do your best with it, and don't neglect those elements of life whose importance the head master has emphasized—music, literature, art. Never was the need of these elements so great in life as to-day. You will find many things in this modern world you will not like; it is hard and mechanical in many ways. And you will want these other elements to maintain those spiritual values, not only for the sanity of your own soul and mine, but that it may radiate from you to the masses of the people. Don't work only for yourselves, but for the good of the community; remembering that, coming from a school like this, you are taking an ideal into the world. Only in that way can you keep enough salt to give savour to the life of our country. And the sanity and idealism of this country are essential for the world's progress.

You will never know what we are suffering from to-day—the losses of the generations of the War. I was forty-seven when the War began, and I saw that slaughter of our men. I have seen from my experience as Prime Minister—looking at the Church of England (where I have great responsibilities of patronage), looking at the legal profession, looking at all the great professions, looking all around the country—that shortage of the men of forty and forty-five who now ought to be coming forward and taking charge of everything in this country. They are not there. And therefore we have to do, perhaps, rather more than our share. And many of us, who would be glad of easing off and handing over, are listening with what patience we can to those who say: "You poor old men, who wants you?"

The world is waiting for you. There will be lots of work for you to do. And if you go into the Civil Service or Politics, there is no

47

greater nor finer work. There is not much financial gain in it; there are many disappointments; but if you do your work in the right spirit, you will find the deepest satisfaction in it.

ON PEACE AND SECURITY

Speech delivered at the Centenary Dinner of the City of London Conservative and Unionist Association, July 2, 1936

I DO NOT KNOW HOW IT MAY BE WITH YOU, Mr. Chairman, but we are much, I think, of an age. I feel I can remember 1836! You were talking about the old firms of the City of London. I will contribute a memory of an old firm in the country. One of my family businesses has been established a long time. In 1836 it was no uncommon thing—as I was told when I was a boy by one of the then partners—to send a bargeful of goods from Worcestershire to Bristol for export or distribution, and a letter would be sent with the goods requesting that a reply might be sent in the empty when it came back. It was possible to do business then and think of what you were doing. I should have been a statesman in

49

those days. To-day we have none of us, either in business or in politics, one minute in which to think.

I am not at all sure that I should have been asked to that first dinner in the City, because while it is quite true, as you said, that 1,100 gentlemen attended that dinner, you had need in those days to be a gentleman of wealth, respectability, and intelligence. I doubt very much whether I could have passed the first standard. The word "respectability" has come down in the world since 1836, and therefore that title might be conceded to me by many of my enemies. As for intelligence, I leave that to you.

But I still think that perhaps one of the pleasantest features of that evening was the flight of oratory in which the young gentleman indulged who spoke towards the end of the evening. In that Liberal City of London he made the most extraordinary and novel observation that Toryism was then sprouting. That may have been a good word at that time. Some years yet had to pass in the political history of this country before Toryism, as we know it, was illuminated, expounded, and made a gospel for a large portion of this country by the genius of Benjamin Disraeli. Most of us who have worked for our great party have founded our beliefs on, and derived our inspiration from that statesman, and we shall be well content if we can pass along to those who follow us something of the spirit of that gospel which he preached. But there was one thing in which Disraeli had a great advantage over us. He lived in an age of comparative leisure. Disraeli and Mr. Gladstone could have gone away for long holidays, and no one would have taken the slightest notice of them.

I have been in office more or less for nearly eighteen years. Feeling rather tired, and not sleeping too well, I took the liberty of absenting myself for the first time in that period for three days, and it has taught me much. I have learned that there was a procession of doctors between London and Chequers. I have learned that the telephone wires were fusing with requests for me to return to London. I have learned that I was breaking up, and that my resignation was imminent. I need hardly say that there is not one word of truth in those statements. No doctor has been to Chequers. The telephone wires have never enjoyed such repose as they have for the last three days, and, though we shall all retire some day, I retire when I think fit. I would only say this—that the first moment that I feel myself to be incapable of sustaining the burden which now rests upon me I shall be prepared to pass it to other hands, and I shall be no light judge of what the requirements of that position are. But, as I say, it is for me to decide, and for no one to dictate to me.

I have sometimes taken the liberty of using myself words that were used on one occasion by a man—not an Englishman—for whom I have a very profound veneration; and that was Abraham Lincoln. Lincoln once observed —for he was subject in his lifetime to no less criticism than I am, and he minded it just about as much—he said:

" I do the very best I can, and I mean to keep on doing it until the end. If the end brings me out all right, what is said against me will not amount to anything, and if the end brings me out wrong [and I would call your attention to these words], ten angels swearing I was right would make no difference."

That is a very profound and very wise observation of a very great man.

Now this is not a night to talk a great deal about politics. No one wants a long speech after dinner, either to make it or to listen to it, but there are just one or two things that I might say to you on what has been happening lately in the wider politics of the international sphere.

As you all know, the Government decided, after much consideration, that they would support at Geneva the raising of " sanctions " which were imposed against Italy in the latter part of last year. We came to that conclusion on several grounds, grounds which, taken altogether, I think are unassailable. You all know, and particularly those of you who have been, and are still, supporters of the League of Nations, the difficulty which has attended the work of that body owing to the absence of some of the greatest powers in the world. You have realized probably, as some of our critics do not yet seem to have done, how impossible it is to effect swiftly and surely, with a League depleted of those nations, what might be done were the League world-wide and universal. The nations of the world, less those great Powers, have done what they can, but the action of the " sanctions " imposed was not swift enough in practice to effect what we had all hoped might be possible, and there came a point when further pressure might well have led to war.

Now we have been called all kinds of names because we have not brought the country to war, and those who have principally criticized us have been those who hitherto have been noted for their pacifist views and not for their support of the strengthening of the arms of this country. You may not know that every day of my life, when I sit at my work in the Cabinet room, I sit under the portrait of a great Prime Minister—the first who bore that title—Sir Robert Walpole, whose great boast was, and whose great reputation rested on, this—that, except on one occasion, he kept his country out of war. There was every kind of intrigue against him to try to get him to break that resolution of his, and to him was attributed that well-known remark, when a war against his will had been forced on him, that the people were now ringing the bells but they would soon be wringing their hands.

War is a very terrible thing, and, when once let loose in Europe, no man can tell how far it will spread, and no man can tell when or how it will stop. I am quite content in these circumstances to be called a coward if I have done what I could, in accordance with the views of every country in Europe, to keep my own people out of war. I learned a lesson last year, and that was this—that, owing to certain developments in Europe, and owing to what I had learned of the practical effect of imposing '' sanctions '' under the Covenant of the League, if this country was again to be prepared to impose " sanctions " against any country, she should not do it with her eyes shut, but she should know that the imposition of " sanctions " might very possibly, very probably, bring in its train war, and, if it was to do that, she must know the facts before she embarked on " sanctions " again, and she must so prepare herself that she could fulfil obligations under the Covenant in any circumstances. That is why we got the mandate at the last General Election which we did, and that is why this country is now preparing herself in the event of its being necessary at any time to take up obligations under the Covenant with whatever may result.

That brings me to another point. The two things, perhaps, are not so far apart as they may seem at first. Your Chairman was wondering why the City of London, once so Liberal, swung round, returned Conservative members, and now gives its almost unanimous support to the National Government. He was good enough to say something of what we hope

the National Government has achieved in the
last five years. But there is a little more to
it than that. The fact that the City of London
supports the present Government might lead
people who do not think to jump to the conclusion that the City of London is against all
progress. That would not be true. There are
as progressive men politically in the City of
London as anywhere else, but the City of
London, from the very nature of its business,
realizes what has always been present in my
mind.

If I have succeeded in accomplishing anything during these last fourteen or fifteen years
I have tried so far as I can to lead this country
into the way of evolutionary progress, but I
have tried to warn it against revolutionary
progress, and I have tried to bring about a
unity of spirit in the nation. I have done that,
not only because it is right in itself, but because one watches this country becoming year
by year more urbanized, more industrialized,
and the potential dangers to this country becoming greater and greater lest at any time and

in any way her communications, the constant
flow of food and of raw materials, might ever
be interrupted. Her life is an artificial life,
and anything that tends to upset it, to break
those cords and those strings, might ruin our
country in a thousandth part of the time it
has taken to build it up. These things are
present in your minds in the City. They are
present, and much else is present. You spoke,
Mr. Chairman, of the amazing progress of
this country in the last five years. That is
true; but that progress, to my mind, can
never rest on secure foundations until others
share it. There can be no such thing in the
long run as the prosperity of an isolated nation.
None of us can see how it is to be done yet—
the fog is too thick—but until the trade of the
world once more begins to move from one
country to another and goods can be ex-
changed and paid for—until that happens there
is no permanency to the security we have
gained.

Does not that bring us back to this, that
while we all know that we have got to go on,

and go on quickly, with this matter of armaments, there is driven into us once more the
mad folly of Europe to-day in the expenditure
she is making on armaments at the sacrifice of
her international trade?   We have to do what
we can in our conversations with foreign
countries to show the folly of this, which, if
protracted too long, may bring ruin to us all.
Therefore we have still to hold on to the faith
that sooner or later it may be possible once
again to discuss the reduction of armaments.
If and when that time comes we must all of
us throw our weight into the effort. This
massing of huge armaments on the Continent,
even the work that we are doing—the money
would be far better used for the progress of
the world.

And be assured that, however difficult things
may look to-day, we have not yet lost heart.
We go to Geneva in the autumn to consider
the future of the League of Nations, how in
the light of the lessons we have learnt this
year we may make another effort to get some
form of securing peace, by collective security.

It is our strongest desire to bring together France and Germany, without whose collaboration no peace in Europe is possible, and I still hope that in these next months we may see some progress to a goal which we all desire, and which we all seek, and which is nowhere more earnestly desired than in the City of London.

Do not be disheartened if critics—whether critics from the Opposition or critics among our own friends—say the Government has no will of its own, and does not know where it is going. Remember this—that in this present age, with events moving at the lightning speed at which they do move, it is not possible to attain your object very often by driving straight ahead. As prudent navigators, we have to go to port or starboard; we have to slow down when we are getting into the ice fields; we may have to reverse our engines when we find rocks ahead; but we know our destination, and though we may not take the direct course, we always have that port in view. Our aim is constant. Our methods may differ according to the seas we are in and according to the winds that blow. But I feel confident that however great our difficulties we shall be judged at any rate with a kindly criticism in the City of London. If you disagree, tell us so straightforwardly, but as long as you feel convinced that we are doing our best in this most difficult time do not withhold from us that generous sympathy that you have shown me to-night, and which means so much to those of us who have to carry what I remember Mr. Asquith once called an intolerable burden.

ON THE UNIVERSITY IDEAL

Speech delivered as President of the Fifth Congress of the Universities of the British Empire, Cambridge, July 14, 1936

IT DEVOLVES ON ME, OCCUPYING THE POSITION of Chancellor of the University of Cambridge —an ancient office, an office of dignity divorced from power—and as President of this Fifth Congress, to offer you the warmest welcome personally and from the University.   Many of you are visiting Cambridge for the first time. I envy you that opportunity.   I often feel as though it were some time in the reign of George III that I visited Cambridge for the first time!   You will see here, let me warn you, if you have not already seen it, in addition to obvious signs of antiquity a spirit of youth, of growth, of vigour, of expansion and of adventure which I think particularly those of you from the newer world will recognize, sympathize with and rejoice in. We in Cambridge are indeed treasurers of a magnificent past, and that past is ever present with us; but at the same time we work for the present and we prepare for and we welcome with open arms the future and all that it has to bring.

I hope you realize how difficult a thing it is for me to leave the field where I generally work and to address the most learned audience in the whole Empire. I feel in some ways more out of place than any of you might feel if you had to address the House of Commons to-night. But, after all, there is a certain similarity in our work. You have asked me to say a few words to you, and you must be patient with me and give me your sympathy.

When I regard the problems that lie before you from all parts of this Kingdom and the Empire, I am impressed by the burden and the responsibility of those tasks no less than I am by my own. For what have you to do? You have to keep abreast with learning in this modern age, in itself no easy task; and you have above all to train the young: an immense responsibility and a position, in my view, of the greatest privilege.

Now, some centuries ago, as may have been recalled to you, Erasmus taught in this University, and there is one extract from his letters which is not without a certain appositeness to-day. He writes:

"I was talking to some of the masters [this was in Cambridge] about the junior teachers. One of them, a great man in his way, exclaimed: 'Who would spend his life in instructing boys if he could earn a living in any other way?' I said that instructing the young was an honest occupation; Christ had not despised children, and no labour was so sure of a return."

That is as true to-day as it was four hundred and thirty years ago.

One or two thoughts come into my mind, however, when I look on these problems of yours from the outside. I have a very strong feeling, and always have had, that the conditions for the efficient performance of that responsible task of yours should be made as favourable as those who control the finances and the direction of Universities can make them. First of all, in my view, men who are doing research, and who have a special talent for that work, which is not common, should be freed as far as possible from teaching. At the same time, I always remember that your work in one way is like mine. You and I are both doing our work in the world for its own sake, and with no object or probability or possibility of becoming rich; and yet I always feel that those who are engaged in your work —I will not speak of my own—should at least be relieved from all financial anxiety, from such financial anxiety as may destroy that peace of mind which is essential, from such household difficulties as destroy the possibility of a proper and a reasonable leisure, and above all—and I think this is true of my profession also—from such a need to augment their income as may draw men from their own proper and peculiar avocation and rank. I think that the importance of a University staff being well paid must be recognized, even if it means employing fewer teachers and even if it means covering less ground, for I believe it is vital to the health, and indeed ultimately to the prosperity, of a University.

Again, going about as I do, and being Chancellor of an ancient Scottish University, St. Andrews, I often feel that something should be done to promote the corporate life in those Universities which have not inherited any time-honoured facilities such as are enjoyed by Oxford and Cambridge. So far as education at a University is concerned—and I am thinking not only of the intellectual type, but of the more ordinary man who often has to carry on the burden of the daily work of this world—that friction of mind with mind which is obtainable in the more corporate communities as opposed to isolation in lodgings is worth a great deal, and is by no means the least important part of the training that we obtain from a University. Though I have no experience of this side, I cannot help feeling that even for those who teach, the bringing together, more closely than is perhaps customary in some places, of those who teach is good for them—good for their minds, good for their pupils and good for the University. I mention this because those who work in the Universities are rather like me: they are not apt to think of or to ask for things for themselves.

I submit these rather random thoughts in the first place to those who, as I said, are responsible for the financial conduct of Universities, and secondly to those many rich men scattered about the world who, perchance, would be only too glad to help, if they could see the way clearly, in the development of the Universities of their countries.

The University ideal not only in this country but throughout the Empire has fortunately flowered and flourished diversely, accepting directions of local energy, and it may be of local climate and of local circumstance, so that we find no two alike. I think the last thing that any of us would want in our Universities is standardization and its concomitant, mass production. After all, freedom, as in politics so in learning and so in Universities, is the very breath of our being. Looking back and from my own experience, I should say that the quintessence of teaching is personality, and personality is about the last thing that can be produced in the mass.

Now, in Cambridge, as probably in every University represented here, we are expanding to meet the needs and the requirements of the age in which we live. When you see our new library, you will realize how much we owe for its foundation and erection to that trust which bears the name of Mr. Rockefeller. You will probably realize, before you have been here long, that the Cavendish Laboratory, famed throughout all the world, owes a great deal in these recent days to a munificent gift from Sir Herbert Austin. I mention these things because, after all, the Universities through the ages and the new ones to-day owe much to benefactors, and I merely quote two out of many in the hope that their tribe may increase!

That leads me to another thought. In these days—it would have seemed strange to us many years ago—our Universities are increasingly dependent on increasing grants from the Government, but that surely makes it all the more important that we should consider with the greatest care how we can lay out to the greatest advantage the funds with which we are entrusted. I doubt whether any University has or ever will have all the money that it wants, or indeed all the money that it could use beneficially; but may there not be some advantage in considering what I know is a difficult and a disputed point, namely, the development of some degree of specialization in Universities? If the advance of knowledge, as it may well be in some places, is to any extent hampered by inadequate financial resources, it seems to me that the Universities must consider among themselves how best they can develop certain subjects and how they may be able, possibly, to exchange students in the event of its being impossible for them to provide for complete instruction in every subject in every University.

This need of growing specialization certainly

69

exists in Great Britain, and I feel that it must exist to some extent in the Empire as a whole. I have been rather straying into regions of University politics, and perhaps I have said enough. I should therefore like, if I may, to change the subject for a moment and get on to ground where I feel that I may speak with a little more authority.

I want to say a word or two about this Cambridge of ours. Cambridge, of course, has as many messages to her sons as she has sons. Perhaps what I took from Cambridge was a memory of her eternal beauty and her eternal spirit, and I want to draw one aspect of her to your notice, to you who perhaps know but little of her and are seeing her, possibly, for the first time. There are many tributary streams to make that great river of knowledge and beauty and tradition and spirit, but all these streams flow from the same source. You probably think of Cambridge primarily as a great scientific and mathematical University. You think of her in connection with Newton and Darwin, and perhaps I may mention also the names of great men living amongst us who need no prefix, because they are too well known for that—J. J. Thomson and Rutherford.

But there is another Cambridge, and, as you wander through our courts, by our little river and through our gardens, do not forget that the *Oxford Book of Verse* might have been written by Cambridge men. The very names are music in your ears—Spenser, Kit Marlowe, Milton, Dryden, Wordsworth, Coleridge, Byron, Tennyson, Herrick, Cowley, Crashaw, Gray, FitzGerald and Rupert Brooke; streams, as I said, from the same academic spring as that from which came Newton, Darwin, Thomson and Rutherford. Their destinies may be different; their source is the same. Their speech may be different—I confess frankly to you that the speech of one of them is unintelligible to me, while the speech of the other is my delight—but even a plain Prime Minister may have noticed, in the last decade or two, some approximation if not an assimilation of poetry and science. Dr. Whitehead

wrote quite recently that Shelley was born a
hundred years too soon, and that had he been
born a hundred years later the twentieth
century might have acclaimed him a Newton
among chemists. Mackail in his *Latin
Literature* said that in the theory of light
Lucretius was in advance of Newton, and in
chemical affinities of Berthollet. Now I take
the view that providence arranged Shelley's
birth at the right time; and I have only one
fault to find with him. There was a man
named Charles Blayds who went from Harrow
to Oxford and changed his name to Charles
Stuart Calverley. He was sent down and
promptly came to Christ's, and we have him
now among our great Cambridge names.
What might have happened had Shelley on
leaving Oxford prematurely done the same!

You know, great poets are scarce. They
are scarcer, perhaps, than great scientific men.
I always feel that one of the tragedies of the
world and of a great deal of modern science
to-day is the way in which the devil is using
the discoveries of the chemists and the dis-

coveries of those men who invented the internal combustion engine for the destruction of mankind. No poet has done that. I do not think many of them did much harm in their lives, and they have left us incalculable benefits for this world. If the Universities can conspire to produce more poets, more power to their elbow —if that be the right organ!

It is not unnatural to one like myself, whose life is spent in the endless adventure of governing men, to turn to the beneficent influence of the poets. After all, did not Horace and Virgil play a great part in moulding the character, the ideals, the ambition and the career of Augustus? And let us never forget that in the mind of Dante—that singular splendour of the Italian race, as Boccaccio called him— there appeared the dream of a United States of Europe. In the time of our grandfathers lived Goethe, a German but a great and good European. No, the poets are of more help to us than the textbooks, and, after all, how little, how cheap is their apparatus! My friend Rutherford, when he wants to do experiments, has to build a house like an elephant house. He requires large sums of money, which I very happily helped to obtain for him, to buy his apparatus. But all you have to do to see life whole is to find a Wordsworth, a few sheets of paper and a pencil, and the miracle happens! I ask you to produce poets in your Universities, poets who will inspire Europe and the world once more with a sense of unity and a sense of freedom.

How discursive all this is! You asked me to say a few words to you and I have said them, and I want to strike one note at the finish which concerns us all. I think it is the case that in every country of the world to-day you find a profound change in the traditional policy of all the old political parties of the State. You find much that is new, or rather very old dressed up as new. It has seemed to me, during these recent years, that the one plain and obvious duty of the statesman who keeps himself true to what he believes to be the genius of his race, is to try as far as he can to keep in the balance the due proportion of discipline and of freedom, with an inclination, if ever in doubt, towards freedom, and to teach his people accordingly. And so I think it is with Universities. Political freedom, freedom of thought, is essential to the maintenance and progress of democracy. We see to-day in some countries attempts to coerce academic opinion. At all costs we will preserve our freedom, but that freedom carries with it responsibilities, responsibilities to which I know that everyone in the Empire will rise. It is not only a question of avoiding bias in teaching; it is far more than that. It means an unusual honesty of thought, it means fairness of criticism and it means freedom from all prejudice—easy things to say; hard, perhaps, always to realize. But we must hold fast to this ideal and to this faith. The world, after all, looks to the British Empire to maintain those traditions which built it up. The light that was lighted in our old Universities centuries ago in this country, the light that has travelled into every country of the Empire, may not yet shine through the world, but we must go on with our work, holding to our ideals and holding this faith, that if we are true to our trust and if we train up the generations to come true to that trust, the day will come sooner or later when that true freedom and the love of God will not only lighten this spot and that on earth but will dissipate the clouds that surround us to-day and will illuminate the whole globe.

ON THE CANADIAN DEAD

Speech delivered to the Canadian Pilgrimage at Westminster Hall, London, July 29, 1936

I WISH IT MIGHT BE GIVEN TO ME TO SPEAK TO you the thoughts that lie deep in all our hearts to-day. You have come from Canada on a pilgrimage—a pious pilgrimage—to visit this old world and those scenes of incomparable heroism which you left nearly twenty years ago, to cement old friendships and to revere and honour those of you who fell. It falls to my lot to welcome you in this city on your homeward journey just before you pay your visit to that most sacred spot, the Cenotaph, in the centre of our Empire, and how fitting it is that I should meet you from Canada in this great Hall of Westminster. Canada was born of two great civilizations from Europe. In this spot you see a building built by a Norman King and in which the first Parliament

77

assembled nearly seven hundred years ago. A Parliament convened by a Frenchman, born in France, with an English heart—Simon de Montfort. Here it is for me in a few minutes just to tell you how all of us here in the old country welcome you with open arms.

We can never forget how in those first phases of the War you in Canada leapt to our side. You stood with us in that first grim fighting around Ypres, and you faced that first gas attack in April, twenty-one years ago. I think we showed you then what we thought of you. We gave you Vimy, the key spot of the whole line. And we gave you moreover Julian Byng, and I think you loved Julian Byng as I know he loved you. When his work with you was done, Canada produced a man, and your own General Currie took over. Julian Byng and General Currie were friends in life, as such men were bound to be: and in death not long divided, for both have been called home within recent years, and each lies honoured for all time in the pleasant land that gave them birth.

78

I remember a few years ago I paid a visit to those wonderful gardens in France and Belgium where our dead lie. I went, as every Worcestershire man is bound to go, to Gheluvelt. I remember walking along that road on which every regiment in the British Army at one time or another marched through the Valley of the Shadow of Death. And I had a consciousness there, which I have never had before or since, that the vibrant air was full of something, and the roads were full, and I seemed to be pushing my way along. I know that that feeling must have been with you at Vimy, that feeling that you were being watched by an unseen cloud of witnesses; and those witnesses are our dead, who are speaking to us to-day. Never can we feel that companionship and that communion more closely than at these solemn moments.

We have often spoken of the losses of the War. That is not peculiar to us. It is common to all countries that took part in the War, and I have no doubt in my own mind that many of the troubles of this world are due to the fact that we have lost our best, and so many of our best, who to-day would be among our leaders. I am confident of this: that if the dead could come back to life to-day there would be no war.

They would never let the younger generation taste what they did. You have all tasted that bitter cup of war. They drank it to the dregs, and even after all these years the dead are doing their work. Within the last few months, for the first time, the French, Germans and ourselves united to preserve the burying places of our dead. On June 8th there was a little conference in London, and the French and Germans laid their colours on our Cenotaph. When men can do that there should be no more fighting; and it was a German who, on that occasion, said he hoped that after the sacrifices of the War, there might be a long period of human comradeship and peace. When you go to the Cenotaph and have a moment of silence and meditation you will think of those who left you in their strength and health twenty years ago, and whom you left on those bloody fields. They will speak to you and give you that message. I would conclude by just saying this to you, that if the world—Europe and the world—can find no other way of settling their disputes than the way of war even now, when we are still finding and burying the bodies of those who fell twenty years ago—if they can find no other way, then the world deserves to perish.

ON THE RENUNCIATION OF
THE THRONE BY KING
EDWARD THE EIGHTH

Speech delivered in the House of Commons,
December 10, 1936

I BEG TO MOVE,

" That His Majesty's most Gracious Message
be now considered."

No more grave message has ever been
received by Parliament and no more difficult,
I may almost say repugnant, task has ever
been imposed upon a Prime Minister.   I would
ask the House, which I know will not be without sympathy for me in my position to-day,
to remember that in this last week I have had
but little time in which to compose a speech for
delivery to-day, so I must tell what I have to
tell truthfully, sincerely and plainly, with no
attempt to dress up or to adorn.   I shall have

little or nothing to say in the way of comment or criticism, or of praise or of blame. I think my best course to-day, and the one that the House would desire, is to tell them, so far as I can, what has passed between His Majesty and myself and what led up to the present situation.

I should like to say at the start that His Majesty as Prince of Wales has honoured me for many years with a friendship which I value, and I know that he would agree with me in saying to you that it was not only a friendship, but, between man and man, a friendship of affection. I would like to tell the House that when we said " Good-bye " on Tuesday night at Fort Belvedere we both knew and felt and said to each other that that friendship, so far from being impaired by the discussions of this last week, bound us more closely together than ever and would last for life.

Now, Sir, the House will want to know how it was that I had my first interview with His Majesty. I may say that His Majesty has been most generous in allowing me to tell the House the pertinent parts of the discussions which took place between us. As the House is aware, I had been ordered in August and September a complete rest which, owing to the kindness of my staff and the consideration of all my colleagues, I was able to enjoy to the full, and when October came, although I had been ordered to take a rest in that month, I felt that I could not in fairness to my work take a further holiday, and I came, as it were, on half-time before the middle of October, and, for the first time since the beginning of August, was in a position to look into things.

There were two things that disquieted me at that moment. There was coming to my office a vast volume of correspondence, mainly at that time from British subjects and American citizens of British origin in the United States of America, from some of the Dominions and from this country, all expressing perturbation and uneasiness at what was then appearing in the American Press. I was aware also that there was in the near future a divorce case coming on, as a result of which I realized that possibly a difficult situation might arise later, and I felt that it was essential that someone should see His Majesty and warn him of the difficult situation that might arise later if occasion was given for a continuation of this kind of gossip and of criticism, and the danger that might come if that gossip and that criticism spread from the other side of the Atlantic to this country. I felt that in the circumstances there was only one man who could speak to him and talk the matter over with him, and that man was the Prime Minister. I felt doubly bound to do it by my duty, as I conceived it, to the country and my duty to him not only as a counsellor, but as a friend. I consulted, I am ashamed to say—and they have forgiven me—none of my colleagues.

I happened to be staying in the neighbourhood of Fort Belvedere about the middle of October, and I ascertained that His Majesty was leaving his house on Sunday, October 18th, to entertain a small shooting party at Sandringham, and that he was leaving on the Sunday afternoon. I telephoned from my friend's house on the Sunday morning and found that he had left earlier than was expected. In those circumstances I communicated with him through his Secretary and stated that I desired to see him—this is the first and only occasion on which I was the one who asked for an interview—that I desired to see him, that the matter was urgent. I told him what it was. I expressed my willingness to come to Sandringham on Tuesday, the 20th, but I said that I thought it wiser, if His Majesty thought fit, to see me at Fort Belvedere, for I was anxious that no one at that time should know of my visit, and that at any rate our first talk should be in complete privacy. The reply came from His Majesty that he would motor back on the Monday, October 19th, to Fort Belvedere, and he would see me on the Tuesday morning. And on the Tuesday morning I saw him.

Sir, I may say, before I proceed to the details of the conversation, that an adviser to the Crown can be of no possible service to his master unless he tells him at all times the truth as he sees it, whether that truth be welcome or not. And let me say here, as I may say several times before I finish, that during those talks, when I look back, there is nothing I have not told His Majesty of which I felt he ought to be aware—nothing. His Majesty's attitude all through has been—let me put it in this way: Never has he shown any sign of offence, of being hurt at anything I have said to him. The whole of our discussions have been carried out, as I have said, with an increase, if possible, of that mutual respect and regard in which we stood. I told His Majesty that I had two great anxieties—one the effect of a continuance of the kind of criticism that at that time was proceeding in the American Press, the effect it would have in the Dominions and particularly in Canada, where it was widespread, the effect it would have in this country.

That was the first anxiety. And then I reminded him of what I had often told him and his brothers in years past. The British Monarchy is a unique institution. The Crown in this country through the centuries has been deprived of many of its prerogatives, but to-day, while that is true, it stands for far more than it ever has done in its history. The importance of its integrity is, beyond all question, far greater than it has ever been, being as it is not only the last link of Empire that is left, but the guarantee in this country, so long as it exists in that integrity, against many evils that have affected and afflicted other countries. There is no man in this country, to whatever party he may belong, who would not subscribe to that. But while this feeling largely depends on the respect that has grown up in the last three generations for the Monarchy, it might not take so long, in face of the kind of criticisms to which it was being exposed, to lose that power far more rapidly than it was built up, and once lost I doubt if anything could restore it.

That was the basis of my talk on that aspect, and I expressed my anxiety and desire, that such criticism should not have cause to go on. I said that in my view no popularity in the long run would weigh against the effect of such criticism. I told His Majesty that I for one had looked forward to his reign being a great reign in a new age—he has so many of the qualities necessary—and that I hoped we should be able to see our hopes realized. I told him I had come—naturally, I was his Prime Minister—but I wanted to talk it over with him as a friend to see if I could help him in this matter. Perhaps I am saying what I should not say here; I have not asked him whether I might say this, but I will say it because I do not think he would mind, and I think it illustrates the basis on which our talks proceeded. He said to me, not once, but many times during those many, many hours we have had together, and especially towards the end, "You and I must settle this matter together; I will not have anyone interfering."

I then pointed out the danger of the divorce proceedings, that if a verdict was given in that case that left the matter in suspense for some time, that period of suspense might be dangerous, because then everyone would be talking, and when once the Press began, as it

must begin some time in this country, a most
difficult situation would arise for me, for him,
and there might well be a danger which both
he and I had seen all through this—I shall
come to that later—and it was one of the
reasons why he wanted to take this action
quickly—that is, that there might be sides
taken and factions grow up in this country
in a matter where no faction ought ever to
exist.

It was on that aspect of the question that we
talked for an hour, and I went away glad that
the ice had been broken, because I knew that
it had to be broken. For some little time we
had no further meetings. I begged His
Majesty to consider all that I had said. I said
that I pressed him for no kind of answer, but
would he consider everything I had said? The
next time I saw him was on Monday,
November 16th. That was at Buckingham
Palace. By that date the decree nisi had been
pronounced in the divorce case. His Majesty
had sent for me on that occasion. I had
meant to see him later in the week, but he had

sent for me first. I felt it my duty to begin the conversation, and I spoke to him for a quarter of an hour or twenty minutes on the question of marriage.

Again, we must remember that the Cabinet had not been in this at all—I had reported to about four of my senior colleagues the conversation at Fort Belvedere. I saw the King on Monday, November 16th, and I began by giving him my view of a possible marriage. I told him that I did not think that a particular marriage was one that would receive the approbation of the country. That marriage would have involved the lady becoming Queen. I did tell His Majesty once that I might be a remnant of the old Victorians, but that my worst enemy would not say of me that I did not know what the reaction of the English people would be to any particular course of action, and I told him that so far as they went I was certain that that would be impracticable. I cannot go further into the details, but that was the substance. I pointed out to him that the position of the King's wife was different

from the position of the wife of any other
citizen in the country; it was part of the price
which the King has to pay. His wife becomes
Queen; the Queen becomes the Queen of the
country; and, therefore, in the choice of a
Queen the voice of the people must be heard.
It is the truth expressed in those lines that may
come to your minds:

> "His will is not his own;
>   For he himself is subject to his birth;
>   He may not, as unvalued persons do,
>   Carve for himself; for on his choice depends
>   The safety and the health of the whole State."

Then His Majesty said to me—I have his permission to state this—that he wanted to tell
me something that he had long wanted to tell
me. He said, "I am going to marry Mrs.
Simpson, and I am prepared to go." I said,
"Sir, this is most grievous news and it is
impossible for me to make any comment on it
to-day." He told the Queen that night; he
told the Duke of York and the Duke of
Gloucester the next day, and the Duke of Kent,
who was out of London, either on the Wednes-

day or the Thursday; and for the rest of the week, so far as I know, he was considering that point.

He sent for me again on Wednesday, November 25th. In the meantime a suggestion had been made to me that a possible compromise might be arranged to avoid those two possibilities that had been seen, first in the distance, and then approaching nearer and nearer. The compromise was that the King should marry, that Parliament should pass an Act enabling the lady to be the King's wife without the position of Queen; and when I saw His Majesty on November 25th he asked me whether that proposition had been put to me, and I said yes. He asked me what I thought of it. I told him that I had not considered it. I said, " I can give you no considered opinion." If he asked me my first reaction informally, my first reaction was that Parliament would never pass such a Bill. But I said that if he desired it I would examine it formally. He said he did so desire. Then I said, " It will mean my putting that formally before the whole Cabinet and communicating with the Prime Ministers of all the Dominions, and was that his wish?'' He told me that it was. I said that I would do it.

On December 2nd the King asked me to go and see him. Again I had intended asking for an audience later that week, because such inquiries as I thought proper to make I had not completed. The inquiries had gone far enough to show that neither in the Dominions nor here would there be any prospect of such legislation being accepted. His Majesty asked me if I could answer his question. I gave him the reply that I was afraid it was impracticable for these reasons. I do want the House to realize this: His Majesty said he was not surprised at that answer. He took my answer with no question and he never recurred to it again. I want the House to realize—because if you can put yourself in His Majesty's place and you know what His Majesty's feelings are, and you know how glad you would have been had this been possible—that he behaved there as a great gentleman; he said no more about it.

The matter was closed. I never heard another word about it from him. The decision was, of course, a formal decision, and that was the only formal decision of any kind taken by the Cabinet until I come to the history of yesterday. When we had finished that conversation, I pointed out that the possible alternatives had been narrowed, and that it really had brought him into the position that he would be placed in a grievous situation between two conflicting loyalties in his own heart—either complete abandonment of the project on which his heart was set, and remaining as King, or doing as he intimated to me that he was prepared to do, in the talk which I have reported, going, and later on contracting that marriage, if it were possible. During the last days, from that day until now, that has been the struggle in which His Majesty has been engaged. We had many talks, and always on the various aspects of this limited problem.

The House must remember—it is difficult to realize—that His Majesty is not a boy,

although he looks so young. We have all
thought of him as our Prince, but he is a
mature man, with wide and great experience
of life and the world, and he always had before
him three, nay, four, things, which in these
conversations at all hours, he repeated again
and again—That if he went he would go with
dignity. He would not allow a situation to
arise in which he could not do that. He
wanted to go with as little disturbance of his
Ministers and his people as possible. He
wished to go in circumstances that would make
the succession of his brother as little difficult
for his brother as possible; and I may say that
any idea to him of what might be called a
King's party was abhorrent. He stayed down
at Fort Belvedere because he said that he was
not coming to London while these things were
in dispute, because of the cheering crowds. I
honour and respect him for the way in which
he behaved at that time.

I have something here which, I think, will
touch the House. It is a pencilled note, sent
to me by His Majesty this morning, and I

have his authority for reading it. It is just scribbled in pencil:

"Duke of York. He and the King have always been on the best of terms as brothers, and the King is confident that the Duke deserves and will receive the support of the whole Empire."

I would say a word or two on the King's position. The King cannot speak for himself. The King has told us that he cannot carry, and does not see his way to carry, these almost intolerable burdens of Kingship without a woman at his side, and we know that. This crisis, if I may use the word, has arisen now rather than later from that very frankness of His Majesty's character which is one of his many attractions. It would have been perfectly possible for His Majesty not to have told me of this at the date when he did, and not to have told me for some months to come. But he realized the damage that might be done in the interval by gossip, rumours and talk, and he made that declaration to me when he did, on purpose to avoid what he felt might be dangerous, not only here but throughout the Empire, to the moral force of the Crown which we are all determined to sustain.

He told me his intentions, and he has never wavered from them. I want the House to understand that. He felt it his duty to take into his anxious consideration all the representations that his advisers might give him and not until he had fully considered them did he make public his decision. There has been no kind of conflict in this matter. My efforts during these last days have been directed, as have the efforts of those most closely round him, in trying to help him to make the choice which he has not made; and we have failed. The King has made his decision to take this moment to send this Gracious Message because of his confident hope that by that he will preserve the unity of this country and of the whole Empire, and avoid those factious differences which might so easily have arisen.

It is impossible, unfortunately, to avoid talking to some extent to-day about oneself. These last days have been days of great strain, but it was a great comfort to me, and I hope it will be to the House, when I was assured before I left him on Tuesday night, by that intimate circle that was with him at the Fort that evening, that I had left nothing undone that I could have done to move him from the decision at which he had arrived, and which he has communicated to us. While there is not a soul among us who will not regret this from the bottom of his heart, there is not a soul here to-day that wants to judge. We are not judges. He has announced his decision. He has told us what he wants us to do, and I think we must close our ranks, and do it.

I have only two other things to say. The House will forgive me for saying now something which I should have said a few minutes ago. I have told them of the circumstances under which I am speaking, and they have been very generous and sympathetic. Yesterday morning when the Cabinet received the King's final and definite answer officially they passed a Minute, and in accordance with it I sent a message to His Majesty, which he has been good enough to permit me to read to the House, with his reply.

" Mr. Baldwin with his humble duty to the King.

" This morning Mr. Baldwin reported to the Cabinet his interview with Your Majesty yesterday and informed his colleagues that Your Majesty then communicated to him informally Your firm and definite intention to renounce the Throne.

" The Cabinet received this statement of Your Majesty's intention with profound regret, and wished Mr. Baldwin to convey to Your Majesty immediately the unanimous feeling of Your Majesty's servants.

" Ministers are reluctant to believe that Your Majesty's resolve is irrevocable, and still venture to hope that before Your Majesty pronounces any formal decision Your Majesty may be pleased to reconsider an intention which must so deeply distress and so vitally affect all Your Majesty's subjects.

" Mr. Baldwin is at once communicating with the Dominion Prime Ministers for the purpose of letting them know that Your Majesty has now made to him the informal intimation of Your Majesty's intention."

His Majesty's reply was received last night.

"The King has received the Prime Minister's letter of the 9th December, 1936, informing him of the views of the Cabinet.
"His Majesty has given the matter his further consideration, but regrets that he is unable to alter his decision."

My last words on that subject are that I am convinced that where I have failed no one could have succeeded. His mind was made up, and those who know His Majesty best will know what that means.

This House to-day is a theatre which is being watched by the whole world. Let us conduct ourselves with that dignity which His Majesty is showing in this hour of his trial. Whatever our regret at the contents of the Message, let us fulfil his wish, do what he asks, and do it with speed. Let no word be spoken to-day that the utterer of that word may regret in days to come, let no word be spoken that causes pain to any soul, and let us not forget to-day the revered and beloved figure of Queen Mary, what all this time has meant to her, and think of her when we have to speak, if speak we must, during this Debate. We have, after all, as the guardians of democracy in this little island, to see that we do our work to maintain the integrity of that democracy and of the monarchy, which, as I said at the beginning of my speech, is now the sole link of our whole Empire and the guardian of our freedom. Let us look forward and remember our country and the trust reposed by our country in this, the House of Commons, and let us rally behind the new King—stand behind him, and help him; and let us hope that, whatever the country may have suffered by what we are passing through, it may soon be repaired and that we may take what steps we can in trying to make this country a better country for all the people in it.

ON THE DEATH OF SIR AUSTEN CHAMBERLAIN

Speech delivered in the House of Commons,
March 17, 1937

IT IS THE PRACTICE OF THIS HOUSE, BEFORE proceeding to the ordinary and sometimes contentious business, on an occasion when we have lost one of our most distinguished Members, to pause for a moment, and for the whole House as a House to pay tribute to that man's life and work. A most painful duty has fallen to my lot on, more than one occasion, and I would indeed that I could have been spared this duty to-day.

It is just twenty-nine years since I entered the House, and on that occasion I had a letter from Austen Chamberlain, whom I knew slightly, and had known slightly for some years, asking if he, as the representative for East Worcestershire, might have the pleasure

of introducing me to this Chamber. I need
not tell the House with what gratitude I, a
young and unknown Member, accepted that
compliment from one who had already held
high office as Chancellor of the Exchequer.
He introduced me, and from that day till now
I have had nothing but kindness and consideration from him through all the changes and
chances of political life; and, though there was
a brief period when there was between us a
fundamental difference of opinion, that, I
rejoice to think to-day, never affected the
regard we had for each other, a regard which,
I believe, existed on his side as it did on mine.
Though there will be one speaking later in this
Debate whose knowledge of him goes back
many years before that time, I felt that I must
just strike that personal note before I say what
I have to say about him. During that period,
of course, our relations changed. At one time
I sat supporting him on the back benches, and
then ultimately he was Foreign Secretary in
the Government that I formed in 1924, where
no man could have had a more loyal and true

colleague than he was, and where he accomplished work for which, I believe, history will give him the credit which I always feel he has scarcely had yet.

Austen Chamberlain was, I think, above all, a very great Parliamentarian. He loved this House. He loved the life of it. He was trained to it. He lived in it, and he has died in it, as I think he would have chosen to do. He was equipped for his task at all points. He was brought up in a hard school at a time when political controversy was raging with an intensity that, in these more calm days, we find difficult to realize; and he learned to play his part among the most effective of those on the bench where he worked. He was always a formidable figure in debate, courteous and chivalrous, but capable of giving hard blows and capable of receiving them. There was never in his whole composition, even through those bitter years before the War, anything of malice, anything underhand; he was the open, chivalrous foe when fighting had to be done, and he never flinched and never lost his courage. I think the whole House was proud of him as a type of a great Parliamentarian. It will seem to all of us the poorer now that we shall never again see him in his place.

It is remarkable to think that, great as his political career was, and numerous as were the great offices which he held, it was during the last years of his life that he exercised in this House a far greater influence than he had ever exercised before. I attribute that partly to this. It is never easy to grow old, but he passed from the position of an active and administrative statesman to the position of what is now called an elder statesman in an extraordinary way. He gradually seemed to drop that partisan character which is essential to some extent to those who are fighting on the Front Benches in the House of Commons, and he displayed prominently those gifts of candour and wisdom which were his. While always ready to criticize if he felt that criticism was necessary, he never criticized for the sake of criticism, and you always felt that, if you had his approval, it was the approval of that honest mind of his, while, if you had not, you might well search yourself to see what you had done to merit it. Many of us, of course, often felt, in listening to him and seeing him, that he was one among us as though he had come from what we sometimes think of as the great days of Parliamentary tradition. We felt that when he left us—and we prayed it might be long before he did so—there would be no one who could take his place. I know that that is often said of men, but with him it is true, because he was powerful in his environment. He has passed away. Yet, do not let the House misunderstand me. Although he was that, and although in so many ways he loved the old ways, and was faithful to them in that studied courtesy of his, in the style of his eloquence, yet there was no man who had a profounder sense of the organic nature of Parliament and confidence in its ability to meet all the changes and chances of life in this country for centuries yet to come.

There is no young man in this House but would say that one of his most remarkable and lovable characteristics was his interest in and his kindness to young men. No one would ever go to him to consult him on any point without his taking the keenest interest in what they were interested in. To no one did it give greater pleasure to hear a young man make a good speech. No one was looking out more eagerly in every quarter of the House to see the men on whose shoulders, in his opinion, the mantle of the great men of the past might descend. His pride in this House, his belief in its capacity, was lifelong. As we know, his conversation used often to turn to the incidents of his younger life in this House. So in these latter days there was no one of the older ones among us to whom I could appeal with more confidence on questions as to how the House of Commons might regard certain actions and certain proposals, or how to deal with a difficult situation. His judgment in those matters was generally unerring, and it was always at the disposal of his friends.

It is for history to relate the accomplishments of our great men and it is for the press of the day to give the facts and the details of their lives. But here we dwell for a short period on the man we knew, and if, indeed, our words spoken here to-day should live at all, they will live for the instruction of those who come after us, to show how a sudden and swift blow could affect the hearts and minds of those who sat with him for so many years. If I wished in a word or two to sum up his characteristics I would say that his chief characteristic may be summed up in that well-known line:

" He reverenced his conscience as his king."

Among the things most deeply embedded in that conscience was a sense of loyalty. That is a word which is used in many senses and is often on men's lips. In Austen Chamberlain I would say that it was the supreme and un-shakable loyalty to everything that he honestly believed to be right and believed to be the best. It was a loyalty that was shown to his family, to his party, to the House of Commons and to his country; and whether it be colleagues, whether it be friends, whether it

be relations, whether it be members of the Civil
Service who gave their service to him in those
many capacities in which he served—each
and all I think would mark out that loyalty
as perhaps the most outstanding characteristic
of his. I have never known him let a man
down; he was always prepared to take the
blame and always prepared to shoulder responsibility.

There is one other characteristic which his
friends will recognize, and again I would quote
a well-known line which may be found quite
close to the one I quoted a few minutes ago:

" He spoke no slander, no, nor listened to it."

I have known him intimately, and I have never
heard him say anything about anyone—
mainly, of course, in discussing political
matters, when feelings often run high—I have
never heard him say anything derogatory
about a man or anything on hearsay or
rumour. Not only that, he was one of those
rare men who are incapable of listening to anything of the kind that anyone may desire to

put before them. It was the reflection of a singularly simple and candid nature, in its best and truest meaning. One remembers, and always will remember those two things, the loyalty not only in action in big things, but loyalty of thought and word where so many of us go wrong.

He has left us. In the remote parts of that countryside where I was born and where old English phrases linger, though they may now be dying, even now I hear among those old people this phrase about those who die: "He has gone home." It was a universal phrase among the old agricultural labourers, whose life was one toil from their earliest days to their last, and I think that that phrase must have arisen from the sense that one day the toil would be over and the rest would come, and that rest, the cessation of toil, wherever that occurred, would be home. So they say "He has gone home."

When our long days of work are over here there is nothing in our oldest customs which so stirs the imagination of the young Member as the cry which goes down the Lobbies, "Who goes home?" Sometimes when I hear it I think of the language of my own countryside and my feeling that for those who have borne the almost insupportable burden of public life there may well be a day when they will be glad to go home. So Austen Chamberlain has gone home. The sympathy of this House from the heart of everyone of us will go out to those who are left. The relationship of father and son is not a thing on which I shall touch here, except to say that no more beautiful relationship ever existed. In all his domestic relationships it was the same—with his wife, with his brother. There is not a soul in this House but will give that sympathy from the bottom of his heart. For us the best thing we can do to honour his memory is to cling more closely to the two things to which he clung throughout his life. He always maintained that public service was the highest career a man could take. In that belief he fitted himself for it and in that belief he worked and died. Let us renew our efforts from to-day to take further pride in this work to which we have been called.

As I said earlier, he had an infinite faith in the Parliamentary system of this country. Let us resolve once more that we can best keep his memory bright by confirming our own resolution that government of the people by the people shall never perish on this earth.

ON TAKING LEAVE OF HIS CONSTITUENCY

Speech delivered to the Bewdley Unionist Association at the Guildhall, Worcester, April 10, 1937

IT WOULD BE AFFECTATION ON MY PART IF I were not to say a few words to you about the peculiar circumstances in which we meet. I remember some years ago, when I was possibly more of a die-hard Tory than I am to-day, and when I had the feelings proper to a young member about the Radical majority which "trampled on our liberties,"—I remember hearing Mr. Asquith speak of the intolerable burden of his office; and I, being young, and never having held office, and naturally believing that all my opponents were humbugs—I felt that was an exaggeration. But I have learned that it is not. And I have known for many years, partly from my own observation, before I held high office, and partly from my own ex-

perience since, that there must be some limit
of time—some term to the period during which
any man can hold continuously this burden.

And I was always resolved, for my own
sake, for the sake of my party and for the sake
of my country, that the moment I felt that I
had given the best of what I had to give, and
felt some doubts as to the future, that moment
I would ask to be relieved of that burden.

It is not fair to your colleagues, to your
successor, to the country, to your constituency,
to give of anything in these great positions but
of your very best. And I do know that the
result of year after year of these responsibilities
is to sap the vitality of the strongest. For in
a democratic country the Prime Minister is not
only the head of the Government; he is the
leader of a party and the leader of the House
of Commons.

To carry on that tripartite task many years
beyond the age I have now reached, is, as I
have said, in my belief beyond the strength
of human nature. It might be possible were
long holidays possible for Prime Ministers, if

they could be seconded for twelve months, and if there could be Prime Ministers in the House of Lords. But none of those things is possible.

We have, in our system, to take these things as they are, and no one but the man who bears that burden is really qualified to know when it will be better for him to ask permission to hand over to someone else than to go on.

I am quite clear in my own mind that, while I believe my judgment to be as good as it has ever been, I am conscious that the vitality is to a certain extent sapped, and one needs more rest, and one gets more tired. But if that be the case in days like this, what right has one to go on with the risk that one may get more tired and really impair the work of the Government of which one is the head?

Far better to go when people may still think of one as, perhaps, not incompetent to do one's work, than to stay until perhaps they know before one does oneself that one is beginning to fail. And so my conscience on that matter is clear, and it may not be so very long before you will have to choose another Member for West Worcestershire.

I cannot help looking back, upon occasions like this, but the last thing I would do would be to bore you with stories of the old days. I would rather look back for a moment, and then by way of contrast point out to you how I regard some of the perils lying before us in the future, that you may think upon some of them as they have been present in my thoughts during recent years.

One contrast, and I could give you no greater, is between the year I was elected and to-day. When I came to Worcester in February, 1908, to meet the Selection Committee who I knew were going to interview me to stand in my father's place, I drove in with a pair of horses from Astley, and took over an hour to do it. To-day I came in a motor-car. Really, there is more potted history in that than is evident at first sight.

I would merely make one observation, and that is this: that, while to-day you may, I believe, drive with safety on the roads at sixty miles an hour, if this country ever tries to travel in constitutional change at sixty miles an hour the Constitution will be wrecked, and it will be wrecked, as it always has been in those rapid changes, in disaster and in bloodshed. That is one more proof of what I have often said, that we must try not to confuse acceleration with civilization because they have really nothing at all to do with one another. There are certain dangers of acceleration on which I may have an opportunity of speaking later, perhaps within the next few days.

The time was in 1908 that I really knew most people in the Division, because I had been about the whole countryside for my father. Since 1892 there was not a village or hamlet I did not know, or a Friendly Society with which I had not dined. I knew them all, and by my side were my father's friends.

I have hardly been down here since the War, except on odd days or a week or two at Christmas, and I do not know my constituents of the younger generation, although of course I know the old ones, and there are many parts of the Bewdley Division who know their Member only through the medium of the illustrated papers. I don't like that, for it makes me feel a stranger in my own home. On those rare occasions that I am at home I realize more than anything that I do not know the younger generation.

I hope I have not let you down, and that I have not destroyed the trust shown in me. I hope very much that you will find someone in whom you can place your confidence. Someone who will be young enough to be with you and the whole division for years, and who will feel the same affection and pride in it as I have. During my office I have been praised far beyond my worth and, equally, been disparaged. But whatever happened in London, your confidence in me has never failed, and it has been a tremendous source of strength to me to know that in this delectable corner of England I have always been welcome.

I wish to say one or two words about other contrasts—about those early days in Parliament and the present day.

I know it is difficult, living in the country-side as you do, to realize the storms and tempests which rage in so many parts of the world and the vibrations of which we in government are conscious both day and night.

In 1908 we were still playing the good old party political game and fighting very largely about Ireland, although at the time when I got into Parliament the question was in abeyance. But because of the political differences between the Tories and Radicals, neither of whom would yield an inch, that was the issue at elections thirty years ago. The natural result was that a solution was found, which, I expect, was the only one possible at the time, though it was one which satisfied no one. To-day there are no issues of that nature, but there are issues just as large in the world, and although I have not spoken much in public on them, I have thought a great deal about them and wish to say a word about them.

I think it may well be a generation or two yet before men—I do not say realize—but properly appreciate historically what the results of the Great War were on the mentality of Europe. Certain it is that we have a phenomenon in Europe to-day new to all of us; a phenomenon that may have been seen at rare intervals in the course of history. In modern history there can have been no such movement of ideas except the period of the Reformation and the French Revolution. And ideas may be very dangerous things.

There is no country in Europe that has a constitution comparable to ours. I do not mean by using that word " comparable " that I am assuming that ours is the best. I merely affirm that they have been all different; that there is no constitution like ours, which has evolved through the centuries into the Constitution as we know it to-day. Therefore it is a more easy matter for ideas to sweep people off their feet in those countries. Throughout the whole of Russia, and of Germany and Italy, you have peoples numbering hundreds of millions who are governed by ideas alien to the ideas which we hold in this country. They are the ideas of Communism and of differing forms of Fascism.

Now, whatever those ideas may produce for those countries, what I want to warn you about is that neither of those ideas can ever do anything to help our country in solving her own constitutional problems. They are exotic to this country. They are alien. You could not graft them on to our system any more than you could graft a Siberian crab on an oak.

But ideas, as I said, can be dangerous. They travel fast, and in those countries they have perfected a machinery for mass impression and mass consciousness. There again I am not criticizing what they do. I only want to affirm my belief that either of these ideas would be a terrible danger for this country. Not that I think this country is in danger of having a mass consciousness. But do not let us, in our happy-go-lucky way, think that such a thing cannot come to Great Britain.

This is a mechanical age. (I hope to say something about that another day.) It is a material age—I have faith to believe less material here than in many places. I hope so; I believe so. But when you get mechanical and materialistic you are going in the right direction to feel the impact of mass suggestion and mass movement. And I do not think there is any single thing more important for our people, and for those who form public opinion, than to keep our people immune, so far as they can be so kept, from the virus of either Communism or Fascism. Our Constitution has been evolved. We have only once within modern times fought each other —at the time of the Civil War. Let us reflect that things such as have occurred in some foreign countries can be brought about safely in no country except by force; and no man who brings about changes by force in any country can maintain himself and the changes he has effected except by the continuation of force, because it is force alone that can dethrone him.

There are some people who speak wildly and loosely about sudden and fundamental changes.

Look out for them, and remember that our party, full of ideas of progress to-day as any other party that exists, has always stood, in Disraeli's words, "for the maintenance of the Constitution."

Those words have a wider application to-day. In my time there has been little that men could say, except some tampering with the House of Lords, that could be called attacking the Constitution. But any attempt at sudden constitutional changes of a fundamental nature would not be maintaining the Constitution; and I hope the whole of our great party and all those who work with us, the great majority in the country, will look out for that one thing. Help the evolution of the Constitution as much as you like; it may well be that things that did for our grandparents would not do for their children, and things that did for us will not do for our children. But the whole virtue of our people, if we have any political virtue, has been the way in which we have adapted ourselves, and adapted the instruments that we use to give effect to our wishes; and we have adapted ourselves without bloodshed and without hatred among ourselves.

Far, far the most important thing that we have to do is to keep this country at least— and it is the only one over which we have control, which people often forget—secure from those strange crises that to-day are rushing round the world.

I do believe this, as I have said to you before, that the influence of our country is very great in the world and in Europe. We cannot keep that influence unless we can make people believe that we can manage our own affairs as decent people. Let us continue to try to do that, and use our influence, so far as we can, for that freedom in which we ourselves believe and which we try to practise, and without which we do not believe life itself would be worth living.

I have spoken to you about as long as I usually do, and I have said something about those many years ago, and I have told you something of what is on my mind with regard to the future. I would like my last words to be once more words of gratitude and words of thanks. I could wish selfishly that we had another one of us to be your servant as the election comes because I am a thorough Tory in that. I wish the connection of the name of Baldwin with West Worcestershire could continue. But after all nothing could stop our association, and I hope by the mercy of God that our connection with the County may be a great deal longer than that of an ephemeral member of Parliament, whether it may be I or anyone else. I thank you for coming in such numbers this afternoon; and I merely say: God bless you, every one.

ON THE STRAIN OF MODERN INDUSTRY

Speech delivered to the Federation of British Industries, London, April 13, 1937

LORD HIRST HAS GIVEN ME MORE THAN MY meed of praise. Many men as a team have been working on our great tasks, and I am just one who by some strange chance has been seconded for special service in the country since the War. Your encouragement of my efforts is an ample reward.

A gathering like this stirs many memories. It will be fifty years next year since I first went to work in an old forge in an old industry in an old part of the country. Many of those with whom I worked were men the names of whose occupations would be strange to most of you. Some were known as puddlers. Few among you to-day will know what puddlers were, but in their day the hardest physical labour in this world was the work of the puddler. Fewer still will know the shingler, who, I believe, is almost extinct. I worked with the last representatives of that great and fine old profession.

To-night I want to speak of some of the changes I have watched in industry during these fifty years—changes which were taking place during the time I was in business, and which have advanced at such an accelerated pace since the War that, if I desired to-morrow to go back to business, I would be of no use to any firm that would wish to employ me. Those who have my memory will agree with me that over that period conditions of work have become easier in works of all kinds, and that they are easier as the consequence largely of machinery. Conditions of work are more favourable in their environment. Much more is known of such matters as lighting and ventilation than was known fifty years ago. Conditions that would then have been deemed tolerable would be intolerable to-day. I think that my friends in the Labour Party would

agree that in many ways conditions to-day are
far less rough for boys and young men going
to the shops than they were fifty years ago.

All that is to the good. But by far the
greatest change to my mind—the most important and most pregnant—is the change of
speed. That affects not only the working man,
but all of us. Speed means an increase in the
rate of production as the result of increasing
mechanization. It is a process which has been
going on for a century, until now craftsman-
ship, which was the pride of our country, has
been largely superseded by the minding of
machines. That is a very great change, and
yet with that change there is no doubt that
there has been such a widening of the market
that a larger supply than ever is needed of men
of skill to build machines and maintain them
when they are built. For good or for evil the
positive creative act of new construction has
given place to the comparative passivity of
watching the automatic machine daily pro-
ducing its interminable repetition of separate
parts. Like all progress, that involves a

whole series of fresh problems, and in industry, as in politics, we are entering seas that are largely uncharted.

The era of speed is yet so young that we know very little of its effects on the human brain or on the human system. Fifty years ago I never remember hearing the phrase "a nervous breakdown." The term was unknown. To-day there is no commoner ailment. It is an ailment common from the chairman of the greatest company in the kingdom down to the workman of the lowest grade. Physical strain, with which the world has been familiar since Adam delved in the Garden of Eden, has given place to nervous strain—a thing far more difficult in its treatment, far more dangerous in its effects—and we know little or nothing about it. Nervous strain comes from the looking after of these great expensive machine-tools, working to the minutest fraction of an inch, and very largely from every kind of modern transport, from driving a heavy lorry along the roads night and day to driving a bus in the streets of London or of Glasgow.

The whole question in my view calls clamantly for study, study by you, study by the leaders of labour, and above all study by the medical profession. The medical profession has been giving attention to these matters. I hope, indeed, that they may regard this question of reaction of the nerves to the speed of life as one of the most vital objects of research that lie before them to-day for the safety of our country and the sanity of our people.

Another thing that we have seen in these fifty years has been the progressive shortening of the hours of labour. We have had the days of the twelve-hour shift, the week of seventy-two, and sometimes eighty-four, hours. We have had the fifty-four and sixty-hour week, and we have the forty-eight hour week or less to-day. My own mills, before I went into the business, were, I believe, the first in the neighbourhood of the Black Country that gave up the twelve-hour shift for the eight-hour shift, but when I went into the business there were older men there who started life under the twelve-hour system. I have never forgotten their description of going to work in an ironworks on the night shift of twelve hours at about eleven or twelve years of age.

It may be that one of the most difficult problems before us in the immediate future will be how far we can wisely reduce existing hours in cases where nervous strain plays a large part in the lives of men. It is a problem that affects not only those present to-night, but those who work for us. It is a problem that is coming very much to the front, and to which many of you, I know, are giving attention. I have no advice to give. I am not qualified. Perhaps no one is qualified to give it. I only say that it is one of the subjects that deserve the keenest scrutiny by those who have the power and the ability to give it, not only among the employers, but among those who represent labour. We require in these changing conditions of the world the best brains possible. It is not so much a question of leisure or wages. It is a question of ensuring that at any rate those people who are in a position where they may suffer from the nervous strain incidental to certain industries may have their health preserved, and not be allowed to become what they may well become if nothing is done, nervous wrecks who are no good to themselves or the country.

It is, in short, a question of what adjustment may be necessary to ensure a sane and healthy life, healthy not only in body but, what is a still more important thing to all of us, in mind. The cheapening effect of mechanization in the production of goods has played a considerable part in the rising standard of life, the rising standard of comfort, and sets no limit to the demand in turn for goods and services. That is of immense benefit to industry. It is said that the human demand is only limited in the matter of food, but even in food it is true that all classes in this country to-day, while they eat less than their forefathers, do demand a greater variety. It is true of all sections, and it gives us a higher standard of life. I mention that because it will remind you of something you must never forget, that our people as a whole cannot enjoy the fruits drawn from the wider world unless we succeed in maintaining a healthy export trade.

That is one of the chief difficulties of the present time. It is going to be a great difficulty in the future, and possibly in the near future. In the past we paid our way by the excellence of our products, the result of the skill of our hands. We were pioneers in many directions in technical production; but there are drawbacks to all progress, and in a mechanized age we must recognize that machinery has enabled the less advanced countries to develop their own industries. In the long run I believe that may be all to the good, because whether it be in the Dominions, or whether it be in foreign countries, the fact that people are carrying on prosperous undertakings will be to our advantage, provided we make the best use of our skill, our brains, our designs, our colour, our art, and our research. It is on that alone that industry in this country can develop to the best advantage. We are to-day in a period of booming trade to the benefit of all sections of our people.

When I say that, there comes into my mind those areas which we call depressed or special. I would pause to say one word about them. That problem is commonly regarded as a problem for the Government. I agree that in a large measure that is true, but it is a problem for industry as well. The Government is doing everything in its power to increase the industrial productiveness of those areas and the lot of the people who live in them, and I think it is up to industry to-day to do its share by backing up our efforts, by promoting wherever possible business enterprise in those districts. I am not asking for this as an act of altruism. I am asking for it as a business proposition. You cannot have a really healthy industrial state of affairs in this country while these black spots remain. Those who may be tempted to think, because their industry and their district are all right, that the misfortunes of their neighbours are not their business are taking in my view not only a wrong, but certainly a very short-sighted, view of the situation.

I come back to the state of the country as a whole. The improved conditions are due to a number of causes. I naturally think the most important was the introduction of the tariff five years ago. Do not let us overlook this fact that owing to the trend of economic nationalism, owing to the adoption of the various devices that have hampered and are hampering our foreign trade, our whole economic structure rests upon a much narrower basis than it did. Therefore, when a turn occurs, it may come more rapidly, and the decline may be more marked. Hence, again, let me impress upon you the necessity of keeping up all our connections that we can in foreign markets, however tempting the home market may be. By developing new production and improved processes we should be ready to take all the openings which must become available as and when conditions improve in the rest of the world, and to the best of my knowledge they are showing signs of improvement.

Another change is concerned with the

relationship of the State to industry as expressed in legislation. When I was young, and before that time, the regulation of the State was mainly regulation to prevent abuses. To-day it has become positive and constructive, perhaps to a greater degree than many people desire. It is seen in such legislation as the Health and Unemployment Insurance, and Trade Board Acts, and many another of that kind. I claim that, unlike the totalitarian States, we have managed to secure both progress and orderly development in industry while still preserving to a large measure individual freedom and our individual enterprise, qualities upon which ultimately all our trade and industry depend. This country owes much also to the steady development of the habit we have acquired of settling conditions of employment by joint negotiations, and to the thorough-going way in which both sides, although strenuously fighting their own part, recognize the obligation to observe settlements when made. In that direction also we have preserved to a large measure the freedom of individuals to co-operate. Their agreements are voluntary agreements. They are not imposed by the State, and their strength lies in the appeal they make on their merits to all concerned to obey them.

Again, there has been a great change in social matters in the last fifty years. There is much less difference in many ways between employers and employed. The standard of clothing has been assimilated, and amusements which half a century ago sharply divided us are to-day largely common to all. The habit of travelling has developed rapidly in all classes, and I hope will continue to develop with the increase in cheap transport facilities. Improvement in housing—in which the Government has played a large part—is another direction in which standards have tended since the War to appreciate. Comfortable housing is an essential condition to the welfare and happiness of the people.

I come back to speed, and I want my last words to be on speed. I see a danger ahead that our people may become mechanized, not

only in body, but mechanized in mind. I
dread the mass mind. I dread the loss of that
independent individualist character which has
made this nation what it is. I dread the
growth of that materialistic view of life which,
to my mind, is a danger both to body and to
soul. We must see to it that in some way we
can preserve the character of our people to
meet the changed conditions of the age, and
see that our character triumphs over our
environment.

You and I have in our separate ways great
problems before us—problems of adjustment.
I must adjust myself to private life, and try
and grow old gracefully without being a
nuisance to anybody. You, with that weight
of responsibility and authority that belongs to
those I see all around me, have perhaps the
harder task of helping to adjust the lives of
your countrymen, the human element of your
countrymen, the minds, the bodies, and the
souls of your countrymen, to this new era of
speed; and may we all of us be rightly guided
in these matters.

ON THE RESPONSIBILITIES
OF EMPIRE

Speech broadcast from London,
April 16, 1937

TEN YEARS AGO I MADE A BROADCAST SPEECH ON the Privilege of Empire: to-night I am to speak on the Responsibilities of Empire. This I regard as a happy coincidence, for the two subjects are complementary, and consideration of the one necessarily involves the other. As responsibility confers privileges, so every privilege brings its own responsibility. In other words, if you expect to receive special treatment from others, you must be prepared to behave in a special way yourselves; if you undertake responsibilities, you may expect a proper reward.

My subject to-night is also appropriate for other reasons. When I spoke ten years ago, barely a year had passed since the Imperial Conference of 1926 had published to the world

the now famous Balfour Declaration, which
defined the relationship to one another of this
country and the Dominions. We could assess,
even at that time, the importance of that
Declaration: what we could not do was to
predict its outcome.

Ten troubled years have passed—years in
which the world as we then knew it has been
strangely altered—years in which shadows
have passed over the security and peace of our
own and other countries. Yet the British
Empire has stood firm. The intervening
years, so far from loosening, have only
strengthened the bonds which hold it together.
If in 1926 it could be said that " the old order
changeth, yielding place to new," in 1937 it
may justly be said that the new order has
triumphantly survived every test.

We may then take stock of that inheritance
which we hold in trust and which, in the fullness of time, we must hand on to our
successors. And it is proper that we should
do so at this time. For soon we are to crown
our King, who is at once the Head of the

Empire and the link which binds its several members together. We shall do so with traditional ceremony, but that ceremony will be adapted to the altered relationship of the various members of our Commonwealth. Joined with us in this solemn act will be representatives of the great Dominions, of India, and of all the Colonies and overseas territories of the Empire.

Moreover, as is customary when the members of a great family come together, a family council will be held—the Imperial Conference. At that Conference representatives of the peoples of the Empire will consider problems of common concern. It is right, therefore, that the peoples themselves, with whom lies the ultimate decision, should address themselves to those problems which may rightly be called the responsibilities of Empire.

For this reason I welcome this series of talks which you will hear during the next few weeks from eminent men of this country, the Dominions and India—a series which I am happy to introduce this evening. That aspect of our responsibilities which I should like to consider is the aspect of spiritual leadership, for, in my view, the British Empire has a solemn duty to the world at this time—a duty which I have described in those words, "spiritual leadership."

When we look round and consider the state of the world to-day, we see on every side bewilderment and doubt. There is no country but has its difficulties; no country but is faced by dangers. I am no pessimist; I believe that in the end the countries of the world will find peace and prosperity—but that road will be a long and a hard one. For such a journey there is need of common effort, of resolution, of endurance; above all, there is need of leadership. No one country—no group of countries —is so qualified to provide that leadership as the British Empire, of which it has been well said: "Free institutions are its lifeblood. Free co-operation is its instrument. Peace, security and progress are among its objects."

And I say this with no idea that we are necessarily better than other people, but because of our experience. For we, the peoples of the Empire, in our relations with one another, have set an example of mutual co-operation in the solution of our problems, such as, I believe, no group of nations has ever before achieved. We have demonstrated to the world in actual practice that difficulties can be resolved by discussion as they cannot be resolved by force. Our representatives meet in conference, not to ratify pronouncements of policy but to exchange ideas, and by discussing these ideas to arrive at the just measure of mutual agreement. In this we find not weakness, but strength. Tolerance creates confidence; and confidence, harmony.

We have shown the world how a system based on these conceptions can serve not only the domestic needs of countries which compose the Commonwealth, but those of the Commonwealth as a whole. May we not hope even to persuade other nations that the method of co-operation would be serviceable on a still wider scale?

Moreover, there is a fundamental difference between the Commonwealth and other political organizations, which should strengthen its power for good—and that is this. The Commonwealth is founded on the conception that war between its component parts is unthinkable, impossible—a conception as striking as it is new to political theory.

So many of our troubles to-day seem to me to arise from the growing materialism of the age we live in. Science has made such advances, and brought such material prosperity and knowledge, that we have tended, as I once put it, " to confuse mere acceleration with civilization." The higher qualities have sometimes given way to the lower—the spiritual to the material. Yet materialism means slavery—slavery of the mind to the things of the body; and slavery in the end means destruction.

The British peoples have always set before them the ideal of freedom, and more than ever to-day it is their duty to maintain and to justify that ideal.

ON LORD GREY OF FALLODON

Speech delivered in unveiling a memorial to Viscount Grey of Fallodon outside the Foreign Office, London, April 27, 1937

WE ARE NOT HERE TO-DAY, AS I TAKE IT, TO assess Edward Grey's place in history; posterity will do that. The value of a man's work can never be made apparent until generations are passed. What we are here for is to leave to posterity some mark of what Grey's contemporaries felt for him as a man. I am proud to stand on this spot where for eleven years he came to his daily task in his office and to speak some words about him, to try to estimate, so far as I can, what kind of a man he was who passed along these ways and trod these passages.

We are here to dedicate a memorial to a great man, a man who was a source of inspiration and strength to all those with whom he worked, a man who will be an inspiration to future generations of statesmen, and a type, to my mind, essential to the preservation of a sane and wholesome public life. Men of Grey's calibre are needed in every generation as a leaven of the whole. In him from the beginning were the germs of future greatness. And what was it that nurtured those germs and ripened them? I think that among the influences of early life we might place high those of George Grey, the grandfather, of Mandell Creighton, and of his first wife. We might place with them all that that part of England, Northumbria, meant to him. If ever there was a statesman made by his environment, personal and natural, it was Grey of Fallodon.

There were two things he said that struck me and seem to me to contain much that help you to understand the man. He said: "I never remember, even in the earliest years, being bored when alone." And he said this, which will go to the heart of every one who was born and reared in the country: "I love the smell of hawthorn, but it is very nearly a nasty smell, and it is now clear to me that the hawthorn, being in nature pure and innocent and full of good intentions, has all but stumbled into a horrible mistake and made a mess of its smell. But it just hasn't.'' A man who could say those two things when still young was already fairly advanced on the road to wisdom. That being so, his native soil, his native rivers, the heart of the countryside and its people appealed to him. His soul was nurtured in such peaceful surroundings, and as a consequence the man was never distracted by the gossip of the market place or by the chatter of the Metropolis. He acquired a poise which in this age is beyond all price.

With wider experience of life there came a constant deepening of the personality and a realization of the essential grandeur of man's character. God fulfils himself in many ways, and it was as though He had said: '' I will show people to what heights the spirit of man can rise.'' He tried Edward Grey as in the fire. Grey had a happy married life for a short time, but he was left alone to face his life's work—the work on which he will ultimately be judged—for eleven years, and in those eleven years he saw everything for which he had fought fall in ruins about him.

He lived to see a new world, a new world full of strife, in mind and in materialism, and all those things that were most hateful to his soul. During those years blindness was coming on. It fell to his lot to marry again, and his wife came to him to lead him by the hand through a growing darkness. She was taken from him, and he was left alone. More than all that, both his homes were burnt to the ground—Fallodon, of which little was spared, and his cottage in Hampshire, so that nothing remained of it. But he emerged of good spirit, with great heart, and with his great soul at peace.

Those who look for spotless honour, for self-lessness, and greatness of service to the nation, find them in Grey, and I think it may well be said by future generations, as has been said of few great men of the past, " How I should have loved to know that man." To know him was our privilege, and on this occasion we do not mourn him. He himself years ago said that death seemed to be going home, and in a beautiful letter which he wrote me in the last few years of his life he said: " But I have had so much of both happiness and sorrow that I feel exhausted, and my mood is one of *Nunc Dimittis*."

Death for him was going home. In Shropshire in the old days there was a beautiful custom in some parts of the county that at a funeral, when the body was approaching the churchyard, the bells broke off their solemn tolling and rang a peal of joy for the sake of the soul that was being borne home. I think that a peal must have rung for him in every church in England on that day. It only remains for me to unveil this memorial to Edward Grey. His ashes are in the north, in his beloved Northumbria; his soul is with his Maker, and his spirit will abide in our hearts for ever.

ON THE HOPE OF PEACE IN
THE MINES

Speech delivered in the House of Commons,
May 5, 1937

I DO NOT MIND CONFESSING THAT WHEN I WAS
first asked to find time for this discussion I
was apprehensive. I have seen so many
occasions, not only in industrial affairs, where
a Debate during a period of negotiation can
do, and sometimes has done, irreparable harm;
but I welcome the temper in which the right
hon. gentleman [Mr. Attlee] has spoken. He
naturally spoke, on occasion, strongly, because
he feels strongly, and because he undoubtedly
represents in what he said the views of all those
who sit behind him. I felt that I would like to
make a contribution to this Debate on two
grounds. First of all, I must confess that,
when the Leader of the Opposition, in a supple-
mentary question he put to me yesterday,

spoke of my interest in democracy, I felt that that was a challenge which the old war-horse could not resist. Again, I felt that, although I was quite conscious that I could not, for reasons which I will give, contribute much argument or much elucidation of what is going on—that is not my primary task—yet I know that my time is short here now, and I felt that I would like once more to say in this House something about things that I have tried to stand for for a great many years. I would like to finish my career here in discussing, I hope in the same temper and with the same point of view, what many older Members must be tired to death of hearing from me.

I do not propose to say much about this particular dispute, and I say that for this reason. I quite appreciate the desire of the Leader of the Opposition that I and some of my colleagues should be in this House and take part in the Debate if necessary; but one of the peculiar features of our free institutions is that we have not the power to coerce people. There have been occasions in my political life when I would have given a great deal to have that power, but I am not sure that other people would have exercised it as wisely as I am sure I should have done, and I have always opposed it. I do not regret not having had it. We may have our opinions, but I am quite certain that, if I were to try to express strongly a particular point of view dealing with a particular incident at this moment, whatever value I might possess—and I hope it is some value in mediation and suasion—I am afraid that that power might be lost. Do not let anyone in this House think for a moment that the Government are indifferent to what is going on; we know too much about it. I have been in daily touch for a long time with my hon. and gallant friend the Minister for Mines, and I would remind the House that the mining industry is the only one that has its own Minister, who was created in accordance with the desire of the industry. There is nothing peculiar in leaving negotiations to him, and he will rise, I hope not too late, in the course of the Debate and give the House all the information that he has, and I think that that information will be satisfactory as far as it goes. I would say at the beginning that I am not without hope that reason will prevail.

I wanted to say a few words to-day on the subject of democracy—it was not introduced by me, but was mentioned by the Leader of the Opposition a few minutes ago—and its relation to our industrial conditions here. I think a right understanding of it is of very vital importance. But I have nothing new to tell the House, and what I say I have said on innumerable platforms. It has not always been reported, but has very often been said at overflow meetings. I have never found an audience of working men indifferent to these matters. I have never had such audiences as those which have listened to such description as I was able to give them of my conception of the democratic State. We all ought to bear in mind, and this has a relevance to industrial disputes, that that democracy in which we all in varying degrees believe is quite the most difficult form of government that has probably ever been devised, and I doubt whether it has ever been achieved in its fullness in any country in the world yet. An autocracy is a very easy form of government, because we all have to do what we are told, and that means that we are saved the trouble of thinking. Under a democracy, every individual in some degree or another has to do his own thinking, and on whether he thinks rightly or wrongly the whole success or failure of that democracy will rest.

When you come to the industrial side of it, this is how it strikes me. I agree very largely with what the Leader of the Opposition said, and absolutely with what he said about collective bargaining. What is the alternative to collective bargaining? There is none except anarchy, and there are rare elements in the country that would like to see anarchy in the trade unions—in my view the most dangerous thing for the country that could happen. Another alternative is force, but we may rule out force in this country, and I would lay it down that, so long as the industrial system

155

remains as it is, collective bargaining is the right thing. I have no doubt about that. And yet we all know in our heart of hearts that it may be a clumsy method of settling disputes, and that the last word has not been spoken. Some day, when we are all fit for a democracy, we shall not need these aids, but certainly for my part, and as long as I can see ahead, unless there is that change in human nature which we are always hoping for, collective bargaining will be a necessity.

But there is another aspect which was touched upon by the Leader of the Opposition and on which I would like to say a word. The world moves very fast, and the problems that we are faced with are immensely intensified and in many ways much less simple than those which our fathers had to face. I will not weary the House again with a description which I think I gave when I was speaking on the Macquisten Bill many years ago, but I pointed out exactly what the Leader of the Opposition pointed out to-day. But I will widen the scope of what he said. You will find in our modern civilization that, just as war has changed from being a struggle between professional armies, with the civilian comparatively uninterested in it, so the weapons of industrial warfare have changed from weapons that affect comparatively small, localized bodies of men, into weapons that affect directly men who have no concern whatever with the issues, except perhaps a natural sympathy with their own class.

Does not that show, just as the dangers of the modern world internationally show, that the one thing we must pray for in this country, not only in our statesmen, but in our leaders of trade unions and in the masters, is wisdom? Wisdom, fortunately, is a thing that is found in all ranks of life; and, equally, the absence of wisdom is found in all ranks of life. I am not going to hurt anyone's feelings, and I think they will never guess what I mean, but I have known disputes where there has been a lack of wisdom on both sides. I will say no more about that. But, after all, does not that show what tests people have to pass to make a success of democracy—what a chance it is for a particular employer or for the particular man who may be chosen as the secretary of a big union? What a chance it is if, in addition to the gifts that make a successful business man and enable him to give valuable service to his union in the discussions which are inevitable and in the fights which are inevitable, he has also the wisdom and humanity that may lead him to a successful peace, a peace with honour, at a time when smaller men might despair. I think that no one in this House could gainsay that for a moment.

I would also say one word, because I want to follow the right hon. gentleman as closely as I can, about one of the protagonists in this dispute, the miners. He spoke, naturally, in very warm terms of men who are both his political friends and men whom he admires, and I think that probably all my friends would agree. Sympathy with the miners now in whatever they may struggle for is not uncommon. But sympathy may not mean much, and sympathy is sometimes tendered in a way that makes people wish to reject it. But I think that in recent years, in spite of all the troubles we have had, there has been a much better understanding among all classes in this country of each other's lives and methods of thought. That was shown very clearly in this House in the Debate which took place not long ago on the Gresford disaster. I think that that Debate showed throughout the House a real understanding of certain aspects of the miner's life, and a sympathy, not of sloppy expression, but arising from that very understanding itself, which is the only sympathy that is worth having. I think that everybody recognizes that. I have always felt that, with regard to the miner's life, we have to remember two things. In an industrial trouble, wherever it may come, never let us think of either of the combatants in abstract terms. All these men and women, on whichever side they are, are human beings just as you and I are, and subject to the same trials, the same difficulties, the same weaknesses and the same temptations.

I think, if you can look on the combatant

armies in that way, it puts you in a much better frame of mind to understand and try in all your doings to administer right justice, in your belief. I was just going to say that while we all recognize, as I do, the dangers of that life —for it is a dangerous life—we also realize that in so many parts of the country, not so much now perhaps as formerly, with modern transport and facilities for moving about, the miner's life is a segregated life among his own people, seeing really very few others—not like a man in a city who is rubbing shoulders with men of a hundred kinds of occupation in the course of a morning. The result of that—it would have that effect on me, if I were a miner —is twofold. First of all, it naturally makes him see his own problems as problems of far greater importance than anything else in the country, and, secondly, it binds him closely with the fellows that he knows so well. The consequence of that is that loyalty of which the right hon. gentleman has spoken, which is perhaps more marked in that great industry than in any other. I never like using the word

" blind loyalty," because that has not a wholly pleasant connotation, but it is a loyalty which asks no questions when once the die is cast. There is something one can admire in that, but at the same time does not that throw a far greater responsibility on the men who have to act and speak for them than if they did not have that confidence?

I get all kinds of letters, some people telling me I am every kind of a fool, others telling me I am rather a great man. They leave me unconcerned. The one letter that really makes me feel rather a fool is when they write and say they trust me so much that they would follow me anywhere. I should not like to be followed in that way by anyone. It is a thought that humbles a man. It is a tremendous responsibility when vast bodies of men are looking to you and are prepared to do anything that you may think right for them. In this particular case there is only a word that I have to say about it, because the right hon. gentleman said all that there was to say, excepting, of course, what my hon. friend will say later. It is a peculiar case, and it is a case which, in an event where you cannot apply coercion, wants very delicate and sympathetic handling. If it is going to be settled, there has to be some face-saving, and wherever there is face-saving again we all know that it may not always be a very pleasant process. I should like to appeal to the House in the course of this Debate while putting forward their views, to refrain from saying things which might make it more difficult than it is. I have, as I say, hope, and I should not say that if I did not feel it. I have known cases where I have not had hope. I have hope because there is nothing here that ought to prevent a settlement with the feeling throughout the country that there is nothing that ought to be allowed to terminate in a stoppage in the facts that are before us. I say that most emphatically.

I am going to add one other remark. I have in my life here made one or two appeals. I made an appeal to my own friends once on the Macquisten Bill. I cannot say that I was sanguine when I made it, but it succeeded.

I am going to make my last appeal in this House, and it is to that little handful of men who can decide whether it is to be peace or strife. There are very few of them, and they will be meeting my hon. friend very shortly again. Fresh invitations have gone out.

Before I make my appeal I have one more observation, again on a point dealt with by the right hon. gentleman. There is no doubt that to-day feeling in totalitarian countries is, or they would like it to be, one of contempt for democracy. Whether it is the feeling of the fox which has lost its brush for his brother who has not I do not know, but it exists. Coupled with that is the idea that a democracy *qua* democracy must be a kind of decadent country in which there is no order, where industrial trouble is the order of the day, and where the people can never keep to a fixed purpose. There is a great deal that is ridiculous in that, but it is a dangerous belief for any country to have of another. There is in the world another feeling. I think you will find this in America, in France, and throughout all

163

our Dominions. It is a sympathy with, and
an admiration for, this country in the way she
came through the great storm, the blizzard,
some years ago, and the way in which she is
progressing, as they believe, with so little industrial strife. They feel that that is a great
thing which marks off our country from other
countries to-day. Except for those who love
industrial strife for its own sake, and they are
but a few, it indeed is the greatest testimony
to my mind that democracy is really function-
ing when her children can see her through these
difficulties, some of which are very real, and
settle them—a far harder thing than to fight.

Having said that I would add this. The
whole world has its eye to-day on London.
The whole world is represented in London, and
they are all coming here to be with us in what,
to the vast majority of our people, will be a
period of rejoicing for many days, culminating
in that age-long service in the Abbey a week
to-day. In the Abbey on this day week our
young King and his Queen, who were called
suddenly and unexpectedly to the most tre-

mendous position on earth, will kneel and
dedicate themselves to the service of their
people, a service which can only be ended by
death. I appeal to that handful of men with
whom rests peace or war to give the best
present to the country that could be given at
that moment, to do the one thing which would
rejoice the hearts of all the people who love
this country, that is, to rend and dissipate this
dark cloud which has gathered over us, and
show the people of the world that this
democracy can still at least practise the arts of
peace in a world of strife.

ON THE CORONATION OF KING
GEORGE THE SIXTH

Speech broadcast from London, May 12, 1937

THIS HAS BEEN A DAY OF PROFOUND EMOTION,
and I am now sitting quietly with two or three
friends in the Cabinet room of No. 10, Down-
ing Street, in the heart of London—a room
which has been occupied by the Prime
Ministers of this country for two hundred
years.

This morning I was in the Abbey. Early
in the afternoon I was privileged to drive in
the procession through miles of London streets.
In the Abbey I saw our young King and his
Queen dedicating their lives to the service of
their people, and, as I said only the other night
in the House of Commons, a service that can
only be ended by death.

And as I drove through the streets of London
and saw the faces of the crowds eager to see

and greet their newly crowned King and Queen, and listened to their ringing cheers, the cheers of the warmest-hearted, kindliest people in the world, I thought there was only one way in which we could all of us make permanent that deep impression of what we have seen and heard this day.

Let us dedicate ourselves—let us dedicate ourselves afresh, if need be—to the service of our fellows, a service in widening circles, service to the home, service to our neighbourhood, to our county, our province, to our country, to the Empire, and to the world. No mere service of our lips, service of our lives, as we know will be the service of our King and Queen. God bless them.

ON THE
BRITISH COMMONWEALTH

*Speech delivered at the Empire Day and Coronation
Banquet of the Combined Empire Societies, London,
May 24, 1937*

NEVER HAS THERE BEEN A GREATER GATHERING
in London or anywhere else than this gathering organized to-night by the combined
Societies. The Dominions, the Colonies,
India are all here, and no greater honour could
fall to the lot of any man than in such company
to propose the toast of " The British Commonwealth." It is a subject almost impossible to
deal with in such a short space of time, but
I think you may allow me perhaps to try and
describe what we in this room represent, and
then to give you some of my own reflections—
the result of many years' work—and speak of
my hopes and my fears.

What that strange urge was that sent men over the seas we cannot tell. It has occurred periodically in history. In Australia and New Zealand they were mostly people of our own blood, and the emigration began at a time when we were going through great distress in this country; but when you look at earlier times and other Dominions, we find that the first to go to Canada were men who brought with them Catholicism and the culture of ancient France, following the footsteps of great French explorers and great French missionaries, and it was only later that the people from these islands moved up to join them. In those days of secular conflict with France it was inevitable that there should have been fighting, but there is nothing more wonderful or auspicious for the future than to remember how, within a generation of the last fight on that soil between the French and English, those two nations combined in Canada to resist all attempts to lower their common flag, and that mutual loyalty has grown and lasted to this day.

And in the case again of Africa, what urge was it that sent men from Europe to so distant and unknown a place? We have to remember that Europe, when that emigration took place, was suffering in ways not dissimilar from to-day. There had been the Thirty Years' War, which had devastated vast areas, the ravaging of the Palatinate, the revocation of the Edict of Nantes, and perhaps it was no wonder that the stern Puritan elements from Holland, from Germany, and from France sought to put as wide a sea between themselves and their old lives as it was possible to do in that day. And therefore they went to seek a territory in which they could practise their own freedom of religion and freedom of life. There they were joined again later by our own people, and again there came fighting, and again there came peace, and again there came a recognition of the common lot of the men who lived on that great Continent, and you have in the South Africa of to-day a united country.

Then we have here representatives of the Colonies, of the Protectorates, and the Mandated Territories from all over the world, but mainly from the tropical countries. You may remember a phrase that occurs in the Covenant of the League of Nations, that the progress and the welfare of such peoples is the sacred trust of civilization, and we shall be judged in the future, as other nations will be judged, by the way that we deal with these vast and fascinating problems. It is no light task, but we have great traditions in our Colonial Service, and in our Colonial Service, as in our Indian Service, we are still able to recruit from among our best, and I hope the time may not be far distant when from the great Dominions of the Empire some of their best men may be drawn to lend a hand in this work, than which there can be no finer work for people of our history and our traditions.

It is a happy thought that as speaker from the Dominions to-night we have our old friend Mr. Mackenzie King, than whom, by his position of seniority among the Prime Ministers and from the history of his own family, no man is better qualified to speak both for that great Dominion and on behalf of the Empire.

I have been a home-keeping man, much occupied in this little island, and have had but a small chance of seeing our Colonial Empire, but we have with us to-night one of my colleagues, my friend Mr. Ormsby-Gore, who probably has more first-hand knowledge of those distant countries than any man living, and can speak of them not only from the angle of Whitehall but from the angle of those countries and territories themselves.

India is an Empire within an Empire. Within itself it contains Principalities to which the attributes of sovereignty are attached. Nowhere has the conception of kingship deeper roots or more traditions or longer history. Many and powerful as have been the dynasties that have ruled in India, none has held a sway so universal and undisputed as that Monarchy of which every man and woman in this room is the servant.

In that loyalty which is focused upon the Crown, India finds that unity that she has sought so long, and we are now engaged in translating that unity into the terms of Federation, from which we hope and believe will arise an India greater than there has ever yet been. It will be largely her responsibility, but I want her to believe, as I know it, the sincerity of the efforts that we have made to help her to this new Constitution. I want her to believe that that sympathy which we feel with her in this great adventure which she is undertaking is a sympathy not confined to Great Britain, but a sympathy which exists in every other part of the Empire. To speak for India we shall have H.H. The Maharajah Gaekwar of Baroda, one of the ruling Princes in India, who has devoted a long life to the service of his State and of India and whose government has been a model for two generations. He is one of the survivors of that great Durbar of sixty years ago when Queen Victoria was proclaimed Empress of India. I should like to tell him that I had a letter only last week from an old friend who must be one of the few ladies now alive who were present at that famous Durbar.

Now, I have only just touched on what comprises the Commonwealth or the Empire, whichever you like to call it, and I think we ought to remember that the Commonwealth or the Empire is the greatest political experiment that has yet been tried in the world—an experiment the success of which may mean much to mankind, the failure of which may mean disaster.

And how are we going to make it a success, how are we going to keep together? The Crown. The Crown is the one tangible link we all know; the link which cannot be broken. If it were, which God forbid, would the Commonwealth hold together? The Commonwealth will want statesmanship in the years to come, and I always felt that when the Statute of Westminster became law, and a new era was opened, the need for the highest form of statesmanship throughout the Empire was imperative.

What are the difficulties? What will keep us together? Can self-interest keep us together? Can trade keep us together? They may all help, that is true. But trade does not necessarily mean friendship. People have quarrelled over trade in the past; they may well do it again.

We want something more profound than trade, and I believe that in the long run we shall not hold together unless we recognize the common ideals, the common inspiration, the common love of freedom of the individual and of the body politic, the pursuit of peace —that peace which now reigns through that vast area of the world which comprises the Empire: and unless we are animated not only by selfish motives of self-preservation but by an ardent desire, of which I have seen traces in the discussions we have already had at this Conference, and which I have never heard before, to help the world as well as ourselves, and so to show our ideals before the world that those ideals may in time triumph.

What qualities do we need? When I say "we," I mean all of us—the Dominions, India, the Colonies. I think there are three predominant—loyalty, sympathy, understanding. Loyalty to our best selves, loyalty to the country in which we live, loyalty to each other, loyalty to the Empire, loyalty to the whole Commonwealth. Sympathy and understanding—none of us have precisely the same problems. Let us each have sympathy and understanding, if we can get it, with each other's problems. Then we shall be less liable to criticism, although criticism in a family I know must be taken as something always existing. Being an only child myself, I was without that form of criticism.

Then I would say, let us dwell, if we can— this is a great platitude, but, after all, a platitude is only a truth that has been repeated so often that people get either tired or annoyed by it—let us concentrate on points of agreement rather than points of difference. It is very easy to do the latter. You never know what the end of that concentration may be. Let us have faith, faith in what we believe, faith in our future, faith in our own country, and faith in one another. These things I believe to be essential.

Now I would like, as but an indifferent historical student, to make an observation about our Constitution. I don't suppose that even the person who most dislikes the use of the word " England " would say that historically England had not been more responsible than any other country for what is now known as the British Constitution, and that Constitution has been evolved through many centuries in this country, and we do know something about it. One of the most interesting features about it historically is that that Constitution was not evolved by logicians. The British Constitution has grown to what it is through the work of men like you and me—just ordinary people who have adapted the government of the country in order to meet the environment of the age in which they lived, and they have always preserved sufficient flexibility to enable that adaptation to be accomplished.

Now that is extremely important, because it seems to me that one of the reasons why our people are alive and flourishing, and have avoided many of the troubles that have fallen to less happy nations, is because we have never been guided by logic in anything we have done.

If you will only do as I have done—study the history of the growth of the Constitution from the time of the Civil War until the Hanoverians came to the Throne—you will see what a country can do without the aid of logic, but with the aid of common sense. Therefore my next point is: Do not let us put any part of our Constitution in a strait waistcoat, because strangulation is the ultimate fate.

And I would say one more thing—don't let us be too keen on definition. I should like to remind you, if I can remind an audience so educated as this, that it was the attempt to define, that split the Christian Church into fragments soon after it came into existence, and it has never recovered from that, and therefore I deduce—and I hope that it is a logical thing—that if we try to define the Constitution too much we may split the Empire into fragments, and it will never come together again.   Politically, if ever a saying was true it is this: " The letter killeth, but the spirit giveth life."

I would like to say one thing in conclusion, and it is something to do with the continuation of the Empire.   I have been at many Imperial Conferences.   I have been in London on many occasions when visitors have come to see us from all over the world, but I have never known such a feeling of the family in London as at this time of the Coronation.   The people have not only opened their doors to you this time, but they have opened their hearts, and you have walked right in, and that feeling of family, I believe, is going to go on right through, whatever our beliefs, wherever we go, whatever our history, wherever we are.   That may prove to be the most binding force between us—the family under the headship of our King.

"THE TORCH I WOULD HAND ON"

Speech delivered to the Empire Rally of Youth,
at the Royal Albert Hall, London, May 18, 1937

I HAVE OFTEN STOOD UPON THIS PLATFORM
facing a great audience, as I face you to-night.
But you are different from any other audience
that I have ever faced. I have presided over
conferences of Elder Statesmen, but you are
a Conference of youth and of the youth of the
Empire. I probably see before me in this hall
potential statesmen, potential divines, potential
poets, potential business men—in fact, the
great men and women of the rising generation.

I have had my hour. I pass soon into the
shade, but for you life lies before you like a
boundless ocean, and the imagination of youth
is busy launching flotillas of dream ships on
its waters. It is not only young men who

dream dreams or old men who see visions.
I have dreams, and I am sure you have
visions. Let us to-night combine our dreams
and our visions—your eagerness, your courage, your strength, and my experience.

In the next quarter of a century as you come
to play your part in the great world, the big
problems will be the problems of Government.
The peoples of the world, disillusioned by the
horrors of war, are all seeking eagerly and
earnestly for what they conceive to be the best
form of Government, under which their
peoples may find happiness and security and
the development of their talents to their best.

So I say to you, take an interest in Government. It sounds dull, but think a minute.
You may not wish to enter politics; you may
have no opportunity; you may have no apti-
tude, no taste. But Governments of whatever
kind tend more and more to influence the lives
of the individual, and if the liberty of the
individual is to be preserved, it is vital that
the individual should know what is going on,
should form his own opinion, and give his

judgment. For that is the foundation of orderly democratic Government.

First, let me say this to you—from to-night onwards and all your lives put your duty first, and think about your rights afterwards. There was a very wise man called Edmund Burke, who lived about five generations ago. He said these words, and I want to give you just three sentences as a text:

> " In order to perform the part of a citizen wisely and well, it is needful carefully to cultivate our minds, to rear to the most perfect vigour and maturity every sort of generous and honest feeling that belongs to our nature. To bring the dispositions that are lovely in private life into the service and conduct of the Commonwealth, so to be patriots and not to forget we are gentlemen. . . . Public life is a situation of power and energy: he trespasses against his duty who sleeps upon his watch, as well as he that goes over to the enemy."

In war, the sentry who sleeps upon his watch is shot. So, you see, a responsibility rests upon each one of you whether you like it or not. Upon some of you it is a responsibility for England; for some it is for Scotland; for some, Wales; for some, Ireland; on some it is for Canada; for some, Australia; for some, New Zealand; and for some, South Africa, or India; or it may be a colony. In fact, your country and, beyond your country, the Empire, of which we are all constituent parts.

When I talk of your country I mean all its activities—everything it comprehends—the well-being and contentment of its people, their education, their religion, their professions, its business, its public affairs, the government of village or town or country, of the province, of the country, and their Parliament.

All that is inevitably committed to you, whether you realize it or desire it or not. As the whole is the sum of its parts, and as you are a part, you are bound to have some influence, good or bad. Whether you live in the country or town, you are bound to have some effect for good or for evil on your neighbourhood and on your country. Do your best by it for your own sake and for the sake of your children.

We are passing. You are the governors of the future. We are passing on to you the duty of guarding and safeguarding what is worthy and worth while in our past, our heritage and our tradition, our honour and all our hopes.

The beauty of the countryside is yours; the green fields and the trees and the wild flowers; the rivers, the moors, the prairies, and the hills; the treasures of the ages in literature and art. All these are yours. All this accumulated wealth, material and moral, is being and will be transferred to your account that you may enjoy it. Certainly enjoy it, but also hold it and, I hope, enhance its value to hand it on.

You are trustees; trustees in every sense of that noble word. What is coming to you is a trust, and not merely a benefit which devolves upon you, a trust you hold for future generations. Unless you rise to the trust there will be little benefit for you or your children to enjoy.

It will be for you to protect democracy in whatever part of the Empire you may live. It must be defended from without, and equally it may have to be defended from within. And it may well be that you will have to save democracy from itself. You have to show the world—and in many parts of it an exceeding critical world—that there is nothing in democracy and its principles, its purposes, or even its methods which necessarily breeds timidity of outlook or mediocrity of achievement.

Courage, discipline, efficiency are as necessary to democracy as they are to any dictatorship, and democracy implies and demands leadership as essentially as any dictatorship, for it is leadership that does not depend on force. It is the leadership of faith and character. Democracy is looking to you to-day for the leadership of the next generation.

I am not going to try to describe to you the shape of things to come. I know far more of the world that was and the world that is than of the world that is to be. Probably all of you were born on this side of the Great Divide, which apportions the lives of all grown-ups into Before and After. I was born on its far side, in the year which saw two symbolic things happen—the publication of Marx's *Capital*, with its gospel of economic fatalism, and Disraeli's extension of the franchise to working men, with its faith in expanding freedom. I mention these two events partly because they are the keys to much of what has happened in the subsequent seventy years, and partly for another reason.

I am not going to dogmatize to-night. Dogmatism is the prerogative of youth. I do not know that many people, old or young, can tell you what is happening around you and what will happen; but I mentioned that fact a few moments ago because I want to ask you, " Who realized in 1867 what the implications of those two events were?" Very few, if any. It is given to few to understand the times in which they live.

Our friend, General Smuts, used this fine phrase: " Humanity has struck its tents and is once more on the march." But it is not yet certain whether it is marching forward to the Promised Land or backward to a wilderness of suffering and sorrow, destruction and death, such as we went through twenty years ago. You were born in the backwash of that overwhelming wave which spread desolation over Europe. Your fathers and brothers who fell fighting in the Great War hoped they were making the world a fairer, sweeter place for you to dwell in. But mankind cannot commit a great sin without paying for it.

The twenty post-War years have shown that war does not settle the account. There is a balance brought forward. When emancipation is achieved a new slavery may begin. The moment of victory may be the beginning of defeat. The days which saw the framing of the League of Nations saw the signing of the Treaty of Versailles. Should both be entered on the credit side?

Twenty years ago we should all have said, " Yes "; to-day the reply would be doubtful, for both have belied the hopes of mankind and given place to disillusion. Freedom for

187

common men, which was to have been the
fruit of victory, is once more in jeopardy in
our own land because it has been taken away
from the common men of other lands.

You may attempt to explain these twenty
years in terms of economics or in terms of
politics; some see only the one, some see only
the other. Some blame the treaty, some the
bankers, some the statesmen, some the dip-
lomats. Some simplify the causes of the
tragedy and make scapegoats of half a dozen
figures prominent on the European stage; but
what is clear is that to-day Europe is neither
at war nor at peace, but stands at armed attention. For every soldier who died at the Front
another stands in his place; for every ship sent
to the bottom of the sea another rides the
waves; for every aeroplane brought down to
earth twenty new ones sail the skies.

That, in itself, is a sufficiently melancholy,
devastating reply to all the efforts of the lovers
of peace. But what is much worse is this:
peace in some quarters is proclaimed as a bad
dream, and war sanctified as an ideal for

rational men. As long as the British Empire lasts we will raise our voices against these false gods.

Let me end, in this the last speech I shall make before a great audience as Prime Minister of this country; let me proclaim my faith, which is the faith of millions of all races from end to end of the British Empire. Here we have ceased to be an island, but we are still an Empire. And what is the secret? Freedom, ordered freedom, within the law, with force in the background and not in the foreground; a society in which authority and freedom are blended in due proportion, in which State and citizen are both ends and means.

It is an Empire organized for peace and for the free development of the individual in and through an infinite variety of voluntary associations. It deifies neither the State nor its rulers. The old doctrine of the divine right of Kings has gone, but we have no intention of erecting in its place a new doctrine of the divine right of States. No State that ever was is worthy of a free man's worship.

The young King and Queen, whom we have delighted to honour in these memorable days, are the servants of the sovereign people. To them, as your chairman told you, they have dedicated themselves. That is the magic of monarchy which is everlasting. The King is the symbol of the union, not only of an Empire, but of a society which is held together by a common view of the fundamental nature of man. It is neither the worship of a tribe nor a class. It is a faith, a value placed upon the individual, derived from the Christian religion.

The Christian State proclaims human personality to be supreme; the servile State denies this. Every compromise with the infinite value of the human soul leads straight back to savagery and the jungle. Expel this truth of our religion, and what follows? The insolence of dominion, and the cruelty of despotism. Denounce religion as the opium of the people, and you swiftly proceed to denounce political liberty and civil liberty as opium. Freedom of speech goes, tolerance follows, and justice is no more.

The fruits of the free spirit of man do not grow in the garden of tyranny. It has been well said that slavery is a weed that grows in every soil. As long as we have the wisdom to keep the sovereign authority of this country as the sanctuary of liberty, the sacred temple consecrated to our common faith, men will turn their faces towards us and draw their breath more freely.

The association of the peoples of the Empire is rooted, and their fellowship is rooted, in this doctrine of the essential dignity of the individual human soul. That is the English secret, however feebly and faintly we have at times and places embraced and obeyed it.

The torch I would hand to you, and ask you to pass from hand to hand along the pathways of the Empire, is a Christian truth rekindled anew in each ardent generation. Use men as ends and never merely as means; and live for the brotherhood of man, which implies the Fatherhood of God. The brotherhood of man to-day is often denied and derided and called foolishness, but it is, in fact, one of the foolish things of the world which God has chosen to confound the wise, and the world is confounded by it daily.

We may evade it, we may deny it; but we shall find no rest for our souls, nor will the world until we acknowledge it as the ultimate wisdom. That is a message I have tried to deliver as Prime Minister in a hundred speeches, and I can think of no better message to give to you to take away to-night than that.